★YOU are SO ★ N★★★ ASHVILLE IF...

the readers of the NASHVILLE SCENE

★YOU
are SO
N★★★
ASHVILLE
by the readers of the
NASHVILLESCENE
IF...

ℝℍℝ RUTLEDGE HILL PRESS®
NASHVILLE, TENNESSEE

Illustration and photography credits: Illustrations on pages 25, 27 by Janet Brooks, based on
original photographs by Richard Crichton. Illustrations on pages 43, 48, 51 by Janet Brooks,
based on original photographs by John McDonough. Photograph on page 153 by Dee Davis.
Photograph on page 153 by Eric England. Photographs on pages 153, 162 by Michael Gomez.
Illustrations on pages 171, 174, 179, 184 by Norris Hall. Illustrations on pages 125, 129, 134,
137, 138, 141 by Mike Harris. Photograph on page 150 by Slick Lawson. Photograph on page
49 by John McDonough. Illustrations on pages 73, 77, 82, 85, 88, 91, 93, 94, 99, 105, 107,
110, 114 by Bill Ross. Photograph on page 153 by Raeanne Rubenstein. Illustrations on pages
13, 15, 16, 19, 57, 58, 61, 67 by Lee Tyler Weidhaas.

Published in Nashville, Tennessee, by Rutledge Hill Press®, Inc.,
211 Seventh Avenue North, Nashville, Tennessee 37219.
Distributed in Canada by H. B. Fenn & Company, Ltd.,
34 Nixon Road, Bolton, Ontario L7E 1W2.

Cover and page design by Elvis Wilson, Hound Dog Studio
Typography by E. T. Lowe, Inc., Nashville, Tennessee

Library of Congress Cataloging-in-Publication Data

You are so Nashville if / the readers of the Nashville scene.
    p. cm.
  ISBN 1-55853-595-0 (pbk.)
  1. Nashville (Tenn.)—Social life and customs—Miscellanea.
I. Nashville scene.
F444.N25Y68   1998
976.8'55—dc21   98-11051
                                                         CIP

Printed in the United States of America

1 2 3 4 5 6 7 8 9—02 01 00 99 98

CONTENTS

Acknowledgments

Many people deserve thanks for making this book possible, among them Ciya and Aisha Whitaker for their typing assistance, Johanna Russ and Jack Silverman for their proofreading assistance, the *Scene*'s anonymous Committee of Insiders for painstakingly reviewing the entries each year, and the fine folks at Rutledge Hill Press for helping to bring this project to fruition.

Introduction

The *Nashville Scene* held its first You Are So Nashville If... contest in 1989. The rules were simple: Readers were simply asked to complete the sentence "You are so Nashville if..." And they were told to enter as many times as they wished.

The contest, I must confess, was not our idea. We "borrowed" the concept from another newspaper, *Style Weekly*, in Richmond, Virginia. The contest generated tremendous reader interest, and hundreds of ballots poured in the first year. The entries showed considerable originality, humor, depth, and knowledge about the city. Since the contest's inception, the You Are So Nashville If... issue has been one of the largest and best-read *Scenes* of the year.

Each year around contest time, a committee of *Nashville Scene* writers and editors—we refer to them obliquely as the Committee of Insiders—reviews the You Are So Nashville If... entries and selects the winners. Over the years, we have learned that the submissions are of two kinds. They either reflect some eternal verity about what it is like to be a Nashvillian, or they are a commentary on some actual event that has taken place in our city during the preceding year.

Whichever category they fall into, we have found most of the winning entries to be side-splittingly hilarious. As well, they have often identified some quintessential element of the city's character, be it our obsession with graciousness, our rage against bad drivers, or our never-ending curiosity about Channel 4's Snowbird. The contest entries over time have shown that we are a city divided geographically: East Nashville versus West Nashville, North versus South. We are also a city preoccupied with class: wealthy Swan Ball-goers versus those who like cornbread with their white beans.

This is not a book by the *Nashville Scene*. It is really the product of *Scene* readers who have taken the time to think about their city and then share their thoughts with us. The credit is all theirs, and we thank them.

—Bruce Dobie, Editor, *Nashville Scene*

★ YOU
are SO ★
N ★★ ASHVILLE
by the readers of the
NASHVILLESCENE IF...

1989

It was not a pretty year in Music City.

Nashville Mayor William Hill "Bill" Boner presided over a city government that was leaking like a sieve. Boner slashed the city's education budget, and class sizes increased from 20 students to 25. To save money, he also cut garbage pickup—and that's when the hollering really started. Nothing, it seemed, could help Boner, even when The Ingram Group, a public relations firm, was hired to put a Band-Aid on the crisis at City Hall.

Meanwhile, in the private sector, the city spiraled into an ugly real estate crisis. The stocks of local banks went into inglorious nosedives, and a large savings and loan—Metropolitan Federal—was on its death bed. Over at the Chamber of Commerce, things got so bad the top administrative official was unceremoniously dumped.

The city's artistic classes, meanwhile, were in mourning. In 1989, Robert Penn Warren, a Vanderbilt graduate and the nation's poet laureate, died. Meanwhile, local moviegoers did cartwheels when they finally got to see *The Last Temptation of Christ*, which previously had been banned by theaters across the city. Unfortunately,

You'd rather have an old name than new money.

Laura Entrekin

The Freemans lost a lot of your money.

Elmore Hill Jr.

You hear someone say "Here's Johnny!"—and you look up to see if June's with him.

Geraldine Hunt

Your vote can be swayed by free BBQ.

Jim Steel

there was considerable grumbling when they had to walk through a line of picketers to buy their tickets.

If the city was in a deep funk, there were upsides nonetheless. Market Street Brewery, the city's first micro-brewery, opened its doors for business. A heart surgeon named Bill Frist wrote a book, called *Transplant*. And a former MBA student wrote a movie based partially on his high school experience. Its title: *Dead Poet's Society*.

In spite of the ill winds, people were at least showing they had a sense of humor. When Hank Hillin announced his plan to run for sheriff against incumbent crook Fate Thomas, he came up with four bywords that would dominate his regime: "Fidelity, honesty, integrity, and dignity." Which prompted one wag to give Sheriff Thomas his own four-word slogan: "Fatback, hominy, grits, and cornbread."

There was hope.

You are so Nashville if...

1st Place

You think our Parthenon is better because the other one fell apart.

— *Susan Fenton*

You drive 20 miles from your neighborhood to buy liquor and meet one of your church members coming out the door of the liquor store.

— *William Colley*

Your curbside trash cans are "done" in hunter green and peach.

—*Kristin Kirkpatrick*

Each year you secretly think about what you would wear if you were suddenly invited to the Swan Ball.

—*Dianne McClendon*

Walking through the Parthenon inspires lyrics of memories of growing up as a coal miner's daughter.

—*Cynthia Woodard*

All your gags, punch lines, and even your philosophy of life hit all the record charts recorded and written by someone else.

—*J.M. Baker*

You shop at Hill's because they don't sell beer.

—*David Ribar*

You have out-of-town tourists ask, "When are they going to finish the top of the TPAC?"

—*Glenda Booker*

The nose you wear is different than the one you were born with.

—*David and Michele Stephens*

Without moving your hair, you can drive your foreign convertible down West End at 180 mph while reading, talking on the phone, and sipping Evian.

—*David Yates*

You know the difference between Broadway, West End, and Harding.

—*Steven Cooper*

Your fiancé made the bachelor party pilgrimage to the Classic Cat.

—*Jim Steel*

You go to the Fairgrounds Flea Market to buy tube socks.

—*Kathy Brady*

Mrs. Rotier has cooked more meals for you than your wife has.

—*Judson Rogers*

You believe-mutuel betting will bring crime and sin to Nashville and destroy our well-constructed moral fiber, and you will bet anyone $100, 10-1, that it will never, as long as you have a voice, come to Nashville.

—*Cheryl Collins*

You dress to the hilt to go to Vanderbilt football games, and you sit in the stadium without seeing more than three minutes of the game itself.

—*Julia Gray Cole*

You register to vote only so you can cast your ballot against horse racing.

—*Beverly Beard*

You can recognize Sarah Cannon without the hat.

—*Gerald W. Dillehay*

You know Demonbreun from Division from Deaderick.

—*Billy Joe King*

You take better care of your flag than you do your wife.

—*Susan Fenton*

The Snowbird predictions send you to Kroger's in a blind panic, where you help clean the shelves of milk, bread, and toilet paper.

—*David Ribar*

You'd rather hire a "Christian lady" for baby-sitting than a French *au pair*.

—*Susan Fenton*

You have an M.B.A. and carry a can to spit in.

—*David Tirpak*

You think Dan Miller and Pat Sajak should trade seats.

—*Susan Fenton*

You have lived here all your life and have never been to the Grand Ole Opry.

—*John Perry*

You pride yourself on Southern hospitality even though you don't know the names of your next-door neighbors.

—*Laura Entrekin*

"25 Names and When to Drop Them" really offended you.

—*Jess Hill*

You think the Tourist Information Center is only for tourists, until one day you can't find East Nashville.

—*Naomi Gothard*

You read Catherine Darnell's column—and believe it.

—*W.R. Mackin*

You long for the Boulevard, would settle for Green Hills, and are stuck in a condo in West Meade.

—*Richard Wright Sr.*

You can't figure out why a place called Music City U.S.A. needs a symphony.

—*Pat Galvin*

Deep down, you'd rather spend 48 hours in Monteagle than a week on Corfu.

—*Susan Van Riper*

Your Mercedes has a license plate that reads BUBBA.

—*Priscilla Fizer*

You think Cheekwood has a better art collection than Fisk.

—*Laura Entrekin*

You'd rather die than have your hair stylist cut off your flip.

—*Peter Fenton*

You think the pope has Wednesday prayer meetings.

—*David Ribar*

You go to church on Sunday, then place a bet on the Monday night game.

—*Glenda Booker*

You know the "Clinic Bowl" is not a lavatory in an infirmary.

—*Gerald W. Dillehay*

You think it's normal for the mayor of a major American city to have as his symbol a dog bone.

—*Billy Joe King*

Your mother can't remember when you started to walk, but her maid can.

—*Laura Entrekin*

Your favorite section of the Sunday *Tennessean* is the Target ads.

—*David Ribar*

1990

In 1990, the city of Nashville didn't need movies, concerts, or the theater.

It had Bill & Traci—that is, Mayor Bill Boner and his girlfriend/soon-to-be-wife, Traci Peel.

The press learned of the relationship and wore the story out. They followed the couple to a downscale tavern, where Peel sang and Boner played the harmonica. They followed the couple into their bedroom—the city's afternoon newspaper reported that Peel claimed Boner was capable of "seven continuous hours" of passion. As the story peaked, the Nashville press joined the couple on the *Donahue* television talk show, where Boner and Peel fielded question after question about what kind of example they were setting for the city.

Nashville held its head in its hands and wept.

Elsewhere, the scene was brutal and ugly as well. Perhaps the most bruising collision of all took place in remote corners of the county, areas the mayor was considering as a possible location for a new landfill. Because of incredible public opposition, he never found a site. With education funding at a low ebb, teachers at Overton High School allowed their students to buy their way out of classes for $2 each. Proceeds were used to buy two new copying machines. Up at the state Capitol, the scene wasn't much better as several lobbyists quietly went to jail amidst a scandal involving bingo games.

In the private sector, people complained of a lack of "leadership." That situation only grew worse when Nashville's leading business-man, Jack Massey, who brought several companies to the New York Stock Exchange, died after a long illness.

But Nashville stayed Nashville-esque: On Super Bowl Sunday, Jerry Sutton, pastor at Two Rivers Baptist Church, threw a party where prayers were offered in place of all the TV ads and fans prayed at halftime. The *Nashville Scene*, as well, tackled an investigative reporting assignment, testing which local restaurant served the most powerful Bloody Mary.

The story proceeded this way: A reporter took samples of the cocktails from six area bars. The paper then had them laboratory-tested to see which drink contained the highest percentage of alcohol. The winner: 12th & Porter, beating out competitors such as Sperry's, Mario's, The Merchants, and T.G.I. Friday's.

When times got bad, you could always go to 12th & Porter.

YOU ARE SO NASHVILLE IF...

1st Place

Your mayor is married and engaged at the same time.

—Maralee Self, Nashville

2nd Place

You can eat Krystals sober.

—Paula Godsey, Nashville

3rd Place

You're sorry Nashville is in a slump, but you were getting a little tired of all the new faces at the grocery store anyway.

—Laura Entrekin, Nashville

Worth Mentioning

You think the school tax hike is another walk for charity.

—Bob Garrett, Nashville

You have a conversation that goes: Dwayne: "His Momma and Daddy were on their way to Babdist to see their new grandbaby and they had a wreck." Reba: "Bless their hearts, are they OK?" Dwayne: "Yeah, but we might could go see them. They'd be tickled to death." Reba: "Where are they at?" Dwayne: "They're fixin' to leave."

—Pam Orlando, Nashville

You simply cannot resist stopping to gawk at ANYTHING on the interstate during peak traffic periods.

—Rosi Caswell, Nashville

Your other car is a Jeep Cherokee.

—Rosi Caswell, Nashville

All of a sudden you don't remember going to any barbecues.

—*Rosi Caswell, Nashville*

You believe the statue of Athena is paganish.

—*Bob Watson, Nashville*

You know the exact place where each road acquires a name change.

—*R. Bluhm, Nashville*

You believe that the new Athena statue at our Parthenon looks like Lulu's bigger sister on *Hee Haw*.

—*George Bushulen, Nashville*

You'd just have to leave town if your Sissy weren't invited to the chocolate for Sara Sue.

—*Mrs. H. Williams*

You wouldn't care how many Metro Council members there were if one would just get some work done.

—*Laura Entrekin, Nashville*

You put a black ribbon on your mailbox when your dog dies.

—*Mary Cate, Nashville*

You're more worried about the demise of the Sure-Shot Rabbit Dinner than what happened to your tax money.

—*Steve Boyer, Nashville*

You think a black comedy is an old *Amos and Andy* rerun.

—*Steve Boyer, Nashville*

You think professional athletes would put Vanderbilt out of business.

—*Steve Boyer, Nashville*

You would fight at least four hours of traffic for 10 minutes of fireworks.
—Ricky McMurtry, Madison

You won't have a party unless you can get Sam.
—Will Akers, Nashville

You don't want any good stores to move here so you can say you buy your clothes in New York and Atlanta.
—Will Akers, Nashville

You have to ask your daddy and you really DO have to ask your daddy.
—Will Akers, Nashville

honorable mentions

You lived on campus at Vanderbilt and thought you went away to school.

Beverly Bruninga, Nashville

"Surf's Up" to you means that Wave Country is open.

Sue Fenton, Madison

You pronounce "Kroger" in the plural.

W. Kelly Fowler, Murfreesboro

★

Your home doubles as a souvenir shop.

Susan Pate, Antioch

You give directions using landmarks that were torn down years ago.

—Will Akers, Nashville

You'd describe a marriage between a Southerner and Northerner as a "mixed" marriage.

—Laura Entrekin, Nashville

You wave for a taxi, and as they pass you, they wave back.

—Debbie Shultz, Old Hickory

Glasnost means America won.

—Adam M. Kroger, Antioch

Suddenly, Ray Blanton doesn't seem so bad after all.

—Jeffrey Jones, Madison

You've actually learned to tolerate the phrase "Have a Jim Dandy Day."

—Kelly Christie, Nashville

You say Nashvulle instead of Nashville.

—Mona Lisa Bradfield, Hermitage

Your house has been for sale for a year and no one has looked at it yet.

—*Laura Entrekin, Nashville*

You buy the Sunday *Tennessean* just for the coupons.

—*Shirley Scott, Murfreesboro*

Someone says, "It was fate," and you think they mean Thomas.

—*Sue Ratliff, Nashville*

You think Fate Thomas is just misunderstood.

—*Adam M. Kroger, Antioch*

You get a DUI and you're not drinking or driving.

—*Jill Smythe, Nashville*

At this point you'd welcome a few Northerners back to town if the bank examiners would just leave.

—*Laura Entrekin, Nashville*

You just normally assume that Fate and Boner are normal names for politicians.

—*Dana Lowe, Nashville*

You can't wait for controversial films to come out on video tape since no theaters will show them.

—Jeffrey Jones, Madison

You call a car pool a hookup, a garden hose a hose pipe, and a cinder block a Breekoblock.

—Martha Lou Deacon, Nashville

A friend saves your life from the deadly current of the Cumberland River.

—Scott Larson, Old Hickory

You don't use your blinker because it's nobody's business where you're going.

—Ross Massey, Nashville

You collected at least 20 pamphlets proclaiming the pope as a Nazi War Criminal Antichrist.

—Ricky McMurtry, Madison

You've stood in line outside the Bluebird Cafe, even on nights you were singing there.

—Scott Gillihan, Nashville

You start listening to country music just to keep up with Carl P. Mayfield.

—Guy Malone, Hermitage

Your school lunch program counted Crisco as a vegetable.

—Joe Gillespie Jr., Joelton

Having a "Boner" is a political experience.

—Mary W. Crichton, Nashville

You look both ways before crossing one-way streets.

—S. Carter, Nashville

You moved here from out of town.

—David W. Alevy, Nashville

You actually laugh along with the Ralph Emery show on WSMV.

—*Andrew Davis, Nashville*

You think the number of KDF-103.3 stickers on your car is proportionate to its resale value.

—*Marta Tetzeli, Nashville*

Everyone who drives slower than you is a moron, faster than you is an idiot, and worse than you is a tourist.

—*Sarah Fussell, Nashville*

You think this is a cosmopolitan area because we have an International House of Pancakes.

—*Diondra Whitman, Nashville*

You think the politician running for a four-year term can still be effective because he's only serving one to three.

—*Kent Chitwood, Nolensville*

When the mayor says he's put in a long, hard eight hours, you know he hasn't been at the office.

—*Patricia Arnold, Nashville*

No matter what table you sit at at a luncheon or banquet, you can find a connection with everyone at the table after asking just two or three questions.

—*Beth Matter, Nashville*

Instead of calling 911 for a police officer, you call Krispy Kreme Doughnuts.

—*Lisa Binkley, Goodlettsville*

You thought the Nashville Knights would be a flop.

—*Michael Gauvin, Hendersonville*

You think Bill Boner is going to give the campaign money back.

—*Vicky Phelps, Nashville*

Your ideal wedding reception includes any or all of the following: a church basement, pastel mints, a lopsided home-made cake... and NO alcohol.

—*Pam Modzelewski, Nashville*

You buy lottery tickets in Kentucky, bet on horses in Alabama, shop in Atlanta, and pay taxes outside Davidson County.

—*Scott Miller, Nashville*

You think the land down under means Georgia.

—*Mike Knowles, Nashville*

You think the expression is "Don't think and drive."

—*Ian S. Campbell, Nashville*

You live across the street from Tanya Tucker and still can't name any of her songs.

—*Dianne Mayo, Nashville*

Your first name is a last name.
> —*Cissy Akers, Nashville*

You were recently a commercial leasing agent.
> —*Norm Ray, Nashville*

You buy symphony tickets but don't go.
> —*Norm Ray, Nashville*

You can drive past any Kinko's in town and not give in to the magnetic-like urge to stop and make a few copies.
> —*Wayne Hogan, Cookeville*

You shop at Stein Mart, but tell everyone you bought it at Cotton Patch.
> —*Cindi Looney, Nashville*

You buy your clothes at Coco or Kyle Taylor.
> —*Richard Courtney, Nashville*

You think *Bull Durham* is a movie about a lawyer.
> —*Sarah Stein, Nashville*

You pronounce "Thank You" as though it were spelled "Thankeeeu!"
> —*Kelly Christie, Nashville*

You no longer question the sanity of someone who says, "It's at Harding and Harding."
> —*Kelly Christie, Nashville*

The "For Sale" sign on your property has been profession-ally landscaped.
> —*William R. Osborne IV, Nashville*

You think the statue of Athena looks like Holly Dunn in hair curlers.
> —*Rich Phillips, Nashville*

Ones we can't explain

YOU ARE SO NASHVILLE IF...

★ You can trace an analogy between the hierarchy, and the catastrophe, which followed: by screening the Table of Contents, set before the "Disciples of Jesus," in the famous painting of the Lord's Supper. Was Judas a pirate?
   Or, there is a proclaim that Judas could have been a paragon, instead of a pirate, in the famous painting "The Last Supper." Also, "Cast your bread upon the Swine" is a connoting after screening the contents of the Table."

★ You weren't I wouldn't be here.

★ Your "Gays" are spoken of as "misnomers" because their accomplishments are "betwixt and between." And if they err, no one lets on. (Thanks to Vanderbilt University.)

★ You bypass the Boar's Head Hot Dogs in the deli at Food Max in favor of the sawdust dogs in the refrigerator section.

★ You can be shopping in Green Hills and run into Hank Williams Jr., and his dad, and know which is which.

★ You go to a sold-out Starwood concert and sit on the grass, and you can't see who is performing.

★ You love the peal of Church Bells on Sun. Morn.—Like the quacking of ducks on a peaceful lake—pause to catch the laughter of children on a busy playground—thrill to the sound of the crack of a baseball bat and ball making contact—appreciate that toe-tapping country music—No Question—You are Nashville.

★ You firmly believe that "He who shall, so shall he who!"

★ While driving down the interstate, you see hallucinatory-looking red lights dangling in mid-air, and slam on your brakes for no apparent reason, nearly killing everyone in your path.

You can be proud of the Parthenon, but ashamed of Athena.
   —*Rhett D. Love, Brentwood*

You feel Mel Perry is ready for prime time on the Christian Broadcast Network.
   —*Brian Russel, Nashville*

You run for city government because you have some home remodeling to do.
   —*Sue Fenton, Madison*

You think E.T. refers to Ernest Tubb.
   —*Sue Fenton, Madison*

You think we should add the Eiffel Tower and the Taj Mahal to our replicas in Centennial Park.
   —*Sue Fenton, Madison*

You are willing to wait 45 minutes to be seated for breakfast at Pancake Pantry.

—*Ira Rogers, Nashville*

The symbolism of the Confederate flag doesn't offend, but the symbolism of Athena does.

—*Sonja Hurst, Nashville*

You think the *Athena Parthenos* really looks like Martha Ingram.

—*Brian Russel, Nashville*

You think Deja Vu is French for "Buck Naked."

—*Brian Russel, Nashville*

You've driven on all of Old Hickory Boulevard.

—*Lynett Alexander, Madison*

You think Lynyrd Skynyrd said it all.

—*Lynett Alexander, Madison*

You wonder when the TPAC building will be finished.

—*Lynett Alexander, Madison*

You think the capitol of Tennessee costs $2.48.

—*Lynett Alexander, Madison*

The prison reminds you of Disneyland.

—*Lynett Alexander, Madison*

U're aginst attacks increese four edgeukashun.

—*Peggy Goldtrap, Madison*

You are not shocked by Tennessee politics.

—*Justin P. Wilson, Nashville*

Glenda Gibbs from Picture Frame Warehouse sounds like a member of your family.

—*Candice Sanders, Nashville*

You have more tattoos than teeth.

—*John Westerlund, Nashville*

You bet against Vanderbilt but hate to.

—*Moe Hill, Nashville*

You're excited about the up-coming Broadway offerings at TPAC.

—*Candice Sanders, Nashville*

You know that an MBA degree comes before and not after college.

—*Moe Hill, Nashville*

You vote the way your church tells you to.

—*Sha Seigenthaler, Nashville*

You believe the *Nashville Scene* is published in Nashville.

—*Bob Garrett, Nashville*

The only Nashville Sounds player you can identify is Skeeter Barnes.

—*Kevin Farris, Nashville*

You're a woman, and you've seen the art deco men's room at the Hermitage Hotel.

—*Jason Goldtrap, Nashville*

You live closer to a church than a convenience store.

—*Lynett Alexander, Madison*

You think scruffy-looking men really go to the public library to read.

—*Peggy Goldtrap, Madison*

You wave to everyone.

—*Lynett Alexander, Madison*

You applaud between move-ments at the Cheekwood sum-mer symphony concerts.

—*Scott Bohart, Nashville*

Crossing the Silliman Evans Bridge from I-65 North, you indistinctly understand that, although the I-65 Birmingham sign directs you to the right toward Memphis and the I-40 Memphis sign directs you to the left toward Birmingham, you are really supposed to crisscross the merging I-40 traffic from Knoxville, take I-40 to the right to Memphis and I-65 to the left to Birmingham, thus avoiding the crashes caused when totally disoriented tourists try to correct, in less than a quarter of a mile, the confusion caused by dyslexic state sign painters. Great Friday after five entertainment.

—*Peggy Goldtrap, Madison*

You've had an affair with Bill Boner.

—*Jason Goldtrap, Nashville*

Your first husband's brother's wife was recently married to one of the former major shareholders of a local insurance company that was taken over, but he didn't have any money left because his second wife was awarded all of the stock in the divorce. (His second wife is now married to your mother's uncle.)

—*Carol L. McCoy, Nashville*

Your favorite ethnic restaurant in town is La Fiesta.

—*Candice Sanders, Nashville*

You remember when 100 Oaks Mall was nice.

—*Jason Goldtrap, Nashville*

You think the seven hour "s....ing" the mayor gave Traci Peel is nothing compared to the one he gave the city.

—*Steve Boyer, Nashville*

Your great-grandfather had a house in East Nashville and so does your daughter, but you live in Green Hills.

—*Candice Sanders, Nashville*

You answer every investment pitch with, "No, you don't understand, I'm in three Freeman deals."

—*Ed Branding, Nashville*

1991

Around the world, all eyes were on the Middle East, where American warplanes were dropping bomb after bomb on the deserts of Iraq. It was no occasion for celebration, but at least one Tennessean was deriving some benefit. After voting for war, then-U.S. Sen. Al Gore Jr. was being mentioned by pundits as an odds-on choice for the Democratic presidential nomination in 1992.

Meanwhile, another Tennessee politician was in the national spotlight. Former Republican Gov. Lamar Alexander accepted President George Bush's call to become education secretary. In reality, though, few Nashvillians had their eyes on national politics. They were more concerned with a mayoral race between former Metro Council member Betty Nixon and health care millionaire Phil Bredesen. Bill Boner, at last, was almost gone.

Fate Thomas, the city's former sheriff, was gone, too, this time to a Texas prison. But he was not forgotten. His wife, Miki, told reporters that Thomas' spirits were high, and he was hoping for an early release. "He said he hoped it would only be a couple of days, because he only had one pair of underwear."

Locally, the city was climbing out of the doldrums. For the first time in over two years, a developer applied for a Metro permit to build apartments in Nashville. The Belle Meade Theater averted demolition by ending its days as a film palace and becoming a bookstore. And Vanderbilt football fans were getting excited about their new, hard-nosed coach, Gerry DiNardo.

In the music world, there were also signs that Music City was being recognized as a creative hotbed. The news program *48 Hours* hung out for several days at the Bluebird Cafe to observe the songwriting scene. Meanwhile, country music sales were beginning to skyrocket.

As well, a restaurant boom was beginning. Sunset Grill opened for business, and became, overnight, a celebrity sensation. Another local eatery, 12th & Porter, made news when a delivery truck from *The Tennessean*, which is located next door, slammed into the restaurant's wall and shut the place down for several days. Meanwhile, meat-and-three denizens mourned the passing of the White Cottage, a 47-year-old institution that was torn down for the widening of the Jefferson Street Bridge.

For some city residents, the biggest news of the year came when a milestone was reached in the arena of civil rights: The Belle Meade Country Club accepted its first Jewish member, Stephen Riven, a partner at Equitable Securities.

Things were looking up indeed.

YOU ARE SO NASHVILLE IF...

1st Place

You say to the person behind the counter at the Hot Stop, "We really kicked y'all's ass in that Desert Storm."

—*Willie D. Sweet Jr.*

2nd Place

The lunch check your daughters persuaded you to sign was really an irrevocable trust.

—*Steve Jager*

3rd Place

The major part of your job is saying, "Thank you, drive around."

—*Bob McLeay*

You're happy when you lose your Boner.

—*Robert Andrews*

You strongly believe that Ralph Emery should (and could) host *The Tonight Show*.

—*Joyce Jessup*

You contribute to WDCN-Channel 8 because it is a Home Shopping Club affiliate.

—*Kaul Williams*

You would have to raise money to file for bankruptcy.

—*Gavin Matlock*

Someone on your street has served as Mayor Boner's press secretary.

—*Charles French*

You get a co-writer to help fill out this form.

—*Lisa Richards*

You're still mad at Shoney's for dropping Big Boy.

—*Bill Mason*

You're still blaming the post office for the slow delivery of your Metro Arts Commission check.

—*Dean Morris*

You litter *and* recycle.
—*Christa Shreffler*

You think Bob Clement is your councilman.

—*John Rumble*

You subscribe to the *Nashville Banner* for its excellent national and international news coverage.

—*Charles French*

You wonder how many mayors it takes to screw in a lightbulb, and then you realize it's not the lightbulbs he's interested in screwing.

—*Hank Williams*

You would rather move somewhere else than "stand up and tell them you're from Nashville."

—*Sara McFadden*

You clean the bed of your truck more often than the sheets on your bed.

—*Lesley Yoder*

You believe it's a feat for a radio station in Nashville to play "four songs in a row."

—*Veronica Wilborn*

You have counted exactly how many times John Seigenthaler has published the story of how he was hit on the head in the Freedom Rides.

—*John Rumble*

Your children contest your will before you die.

—*Penny Phillips*

You think Garth Brooks' hat fits.

—Mike Milligan

You've seen the traffic violation film so many times you give it two thumbs up.

—Cayce Clay

You've never made a left turn off Charlotte while going downtown.

—Christa Shreffler

You're for public smoking but against public kissing.

—Frank Russell

honorable mentions

Your first name is your grandfather's last name, your last name is your grandson's first name, and all three of you are called Bud.

Ron Kidd

You always went to drive-in movies in the trunk.

Rita Gayle Bryant

You ask all new acquaintances what church they belong to.

Mary Carter

You wish Fan Fair would move to Branson, Missouri.

—Rick Cordell

You hold your breath when stopped by a Metro policeman.

—Traci Hollis

You personally know all the people who advertise on Lightning 100.

—Donna Howley-Orr

The yellow ribbon that is tied on your mailbox to show your support for the troops in the Gulf says, "Police Line: Do Not Cross." (I actually saw this.)

—Claudia Lindsey

You put on your tennis outfit to go to lunch at the Corner Market.

—Karen McKinney

You think the Ten Commandments don't apply on Dickerson Road.

—Justin Wilson

Summer Lights still owes you money.

—*David Findley*

Your attorney filed bankruptcy for himself before he could file for you.

—*John Hasenfuss*

You actually want to be seen at the Stock-Yard.

—*Bonnie Thornton*

You've been wondering why the Legislature's parking garage, paid for by the taxpayers, is off limits to the public even when the morons aren't in session.

—*John Lomax III*

You haven't realized that the collective IQ of our state and city political leadership is exceeded by that of a single lobotomized angleworm.

—*Dale Robertson*

Your downtown can burn trash and render livestock.

—*Sherry Thompson*

It's a tough choice for you between hair spray and an ozone layer.

—*Frank Russell*

You think building roads in a circle is logical.

—*Judith Bark*

You wonder why Teddy Bart never sings anymore.

—*Bill Mason*

Your church choir has a booking agent.

—*Bob Barrett and Jim Hennessey*

You're torn between taking your husband's name or keeping your daddy's.

—*Christa Shreffler*

You had to be there

Some entries we have a difficult time grasping. Perhaps you can figure them out. But then, maybe we don't need to know. Names withheld for obvious reasons.

YOU ARE SO NASHVILLE IF...

★ You see a human being making love to a horse and that person turns to you and smiles. (This really happened in 1988 when I first stepped foot in Nashville, coming from Florida.)

★ You've ever gotten fleas or lice from your massage therapist.

★ You attend services with Dr. Omega, 488 Lamont Drive, Apt. Q-258.

★ You make it through the day without being shot.

★ You know the wages of sin are death, but by the time the governor takes the taxes out, it'll just be a tired feeling.

★ You go straight from your wedding ceremony to a no-reservations-accepted restaurant without opting to change clothes, thinking that it is cute (and not at all pathetic) to sit on a crowded bench in Chili's on Murfreesboro Road in a big, shiny, full-length dress and veil while waiting for your name to be called, then drag your train across the food-splattered, cigarette butt-littered floor on the way to your table.

* You know the name of the fat, yellow dog who lives on the corner of 24th Avenue and Blair Boulevard.

* Your son or daughter brings a friend over for dinner and you tell them not to bring them back anymore.

* In an attempt to be accident-free, you cautiously drive 10 mph below the posted speed limit, creating a bottleneck behind you that causes a wreck which ties up traffic for hours while you're out at Shoney's and gives you something to slow down and stare at.

* You wish Alabama's area code were something other than 205.

You get your car loan from the Church of Christ.

—*Kathy Pennington*

You love using I-440 and don't recall ever opposing it.

—*Paul Felton*

You like the smell of your tap water.

—*S. Kearns*

You still wonder where Tom Siler went.

—*Tina Henry*

You tell your wife you go to Hooters just to play volleyball.

—*Jade and Tony Nowak*

You're proud that Pat Sajak once worked in Nashville.

—*Tina Henry*

You already miss Bill and Traci.

—*Don Wirth*

honorable mentions

You gave money to David Lipscomb and had to borrow it back.

Haywood Moxley

You are on the UFO welcoming committee.

Lisa Abraham

It weren't for telemarketing, your friends would never call you.

—*Bryce Coatney*

Your throat doctor allows you to sing for fans but not talk to them.

—*Kaul Williams*

You believe that you'll be able to view luggage on display at a fashion designer's trunk show.

—*Barry Joshua Grider*

The sight of Francis E. Carter's quivering chins is forever etched in your memory.

—*Carey Moore*

You know the best directions to anywhere in town are "turn right at Kroger, then left at the Church of Christ."

—*Bobby Braddock*

Your wife used to wake up actually thinking of ways to get rid of a boner.

—*David Weyand*

You still follow Dan Miller's career.

—Diane and Elliot Greenberg

You make it a rule to beat your children only at Wal-Mart.

—Bill Mason

You can remember where everything was but you don't know where anything is.

—Fredrick Strobel

You've fired a journalist in the last 12 months.

—Gary Coffey

You think Jim (Ernest) Varney is a "performance artist."

—Robert Mead

Six guests came to your Halloween party in Bill Boner costumes.

—Susan Morris

Every conversation has at least one "okey-dokey" in it.

Judith Bark

You point out, when selling the car, that the turn signals have never been used.

Colleen Patterson

You've been trying to decide whether to side with Lee and Sally Beaman or the girls.

Jan Bell

The first ingredient you think of for salad is Jell-O.

John Kuner

You have yourself paged at Sperry's.

—*Carey Moore*

The only art you recognize comes in small, medium, or large.

—*Jerry Brown*

Your hair keeps getting caught on the sun visor of your Trans Am.

—*Bitsy Weaver*

You dress to complement your tattoo.

—*Lisa Abraham*

You think "politically correct" means voting Republican.

—*Judith Bark*

You think it's normal that your councilman is also a paid lobbyist.

—*Tony Rairden*

You own at least one duck decoy lamp.

—*Don Wirth*

You think Traci Peel is a Soviet secret agent bent on destroying Nashville's economy.

—*Gavin Matlock*

Your hair is too big to permit access to some of the rides at Opryland.

—*Karen McKinney*

You wish minimum wage would go up 'cause you need the extra cash.

—*John Hackett and Angela Newsom*

You recently received your fifth traffic citation for not having a bumper.

—*John Rumble*

This is your brain... V.U. ... and this is your brain on drugs... U.T.

—*Ray Lynn Wood*

You don't think of Gidget and a chipmunk when you hear the names Sally and Alvin.

—*Pamela Cheney*

honorable mentions

Your Mercedes has a wreath on its grill for the holidays.

Don Wirth

You think old graveyards with damaged headstones should be restored, but old graveyards with no headstones should be landfills.

Kevin Barbieux

The Sweetest Entries

We bring you these entries because, while they are not in a category with the other winners, they contain so much heart-dripping love and unquestioning affection that they provide a special joy all their own.

YOU ARE SO NASHVILLE IF...

You can enjoy very special friends and all the true beauty and scenery and the beautiful flowers at the Opryland Hotel.

—Gloria Rossiter

You remember Sulphur Dell, the Nashville Vols, and the first Shoney's with curb service.

—Ben Moore

Even though you've never met him, you love Jerry Thompson's column, have followed his health problems, wish him only the best and a quick recovery again, and feel he's your friend.

—Kelly and Bill Christie

You realize we have the prettiest girls in the country.

—Kelly and Bill Christie

You can say you've been to the Opry several times and have marveled at the Parthenon's unique design, but if you've helped a wandering tourist, then that makes you a "So Nashville If" purist and apart from other Nashvillians, oh how you do shine!!!

—Andy Hageman

You secretly covet a Bill Hall Sunshine Award.

—*Denise Volz*

You think record producers and publishers actually go to writers' nights.

—*Betsy Dodd*

Target is OK, but Kmart is not.

—*Lisa Abraham*

The highlight of your evening is to see the results of Channel 5's "Telepoll" on the 10 p.m. news.

—*Alan Herbers*

A car going sideways up an icy hill looks perfectly normal to you.

—*David and Patricia Hampton*

You wonder which three are the Ugly Ones at Deja Vu.

—*Jade and Tony Nowak*

1992

There were flops and there were fizzles, but in the end, the glitter of Music Row pulled the city through.

In January, *The New York Times* ran a lengthy story on the growing popularity of country music, complete with descriptions of music biz luncheons at Sunset Grill and the fortunes being made on Music Row. It was as if Nashville were becoming the Third Coast.

Never mind that, in the state legislature, lawmakers had rebuffed Gov. Ned McWherter's well-considered plea for tax reform. Never mind that, in a lifestyles survey taken by the Nashville Area Chamber of Commerce, Nashvillians declared some of their top activities to be "Bible and devotional reading," "entering sweepstakes," and "sewing."

Over on Music Row and in other parts of the city, we were on a cosmopolitan upswing. Jimmy Bowen, who was running Capitol Nashville's record division, declared that with all the money Garth Brooks was making for him, he planned to start producing jazz, new age, and pop sessions. Promoters were crowing that people like Jimmy Buffett, Steve Winwood, and Janis Ian were calling Music City home. Nashville, it seemed, was becoming more than just country. "More of the right people are here than ever before," commented Bill Ivey, director of the Country Music Hall of Fame.

But the city was finding itself at the center of other whirlwinds too. Local politico John Jay Hooker began imploring Ross Perot to consider running for president. And sure enough, Perot ran. Meanwhile, as presidential candidate Bill Clinton found himself hounded by allegations of draft-dodging and pot-smoking, people pleaded with our own Al Gore to run. Sure enough, he did—as Clinton's vice presidential candidate.

On the religious front, a new Jewish congregation was formed. Congregation Micah was founded when some congregants at The Temple were concerned that their rabbi, Stephen Fuchs, would not perform interdenominational marriages.

Perhaps the worst news locally involved a black Metro police officer, Reginald Miller, who was dragged from his car and roughed up by his fellow officers. Miller, not wearing a uniform at the time, claimed the incident was racially motivated. Outraged black leaders called for a boycott of the city by conventioneers.

Meanwhile, the most cogent analysis of the city came when three-time Formula One car racing champion Jackie Stewart came to town on a promotional tour. Talking to a reporter, he complained about the local drivers. "You people tailgate," he said.

Some truths, it seemed, were eternal.

YOU ARE SO NASHVILLE IF...

1st Place

You go to a Hank Williams Jr. concert at Starwood and pass out before Hank does.

—*Ted W. Davis III, Nashville*

2nd Place

You log at least 26 hours a year standing in line at the Pancake Pantry.

—*Lory Montgomery, Nashville*

3rd Place

You think Greenpeace is a lawn service.

—*Melissa K. English*

You think that a coming-out party is the celebration held when your favorite political candidate is released from prison.

—*Somer Hooker, Brentwood*

Your attorney advertises in the *Thrifty Nickel*.

> —*Jeffrey Spark, Nashville*

You don't care what they say, Tipper never boogied to "Louie Louie...."

> —*Steve Meigs, Nashville*

You are a musician and are currently working on a song called "Would You Like Fries With That?"

> —*Shelia Lorenz, Murfreesboro*

You secretly hope that an earthquake destroys Memphis because we deserved a Hard Rock Cafe.

> —*Terry Robertson, Nashville*

You know how to use Ellington Parkway.

> —*Suzy Ward, Nashville*

You can facilitate in the Gold Rush restrooms!

—*Carla Medlock, Goodlettsville*

You meet someone from another state and ask, "Do you know my friend (friend's name here), he's from there."

—*Mitzi Riley, Nashville*

After casually being asked if you're a Protestant, you indignantly snap, chest puffed out in pride, "Hell no! I'm Church of Christ!"

—*Royce McCrary, Hermitage*

You believed that putting awnings on Hap Towne's was a big deal.

—*Anne Simmons, Nashville*

You miss Ralph Emery a lot more than you thought you would.

—*Scott Gillihan, Nashville*

You wait for a holiday weekend to see how many of your college friends appear in night court.

—*Carlton Bell, Nashville*

You actually noticed and cried when Ralph Emery retired from his morning show.

—*Amy Hollander, Nashville*

You are a songwriter who moved here hoping to make it as a waiter.

—*Bill Guler, Nashville*

You go to a jazz performance where the audience is 98 percent white and you don't notice that something is wrong.

—*Martha Graham, Nashville*

You collect Bill Hall's gardening segments on home video.

—*Jim Clark, Nashville*

You are still kicking yourself for not voting Phil Bredesen into office four years ago.

—Charles Sowells, Nashville

You serve Jogging in a Jug in Waterford crystal.

—Nancye Willis, Nashville

You think the passengers on the bus who are speaking in a foreign language are talking about you.

—Catherine Cunningham, Nashville

You go to a Patsy Cline Memorial Show expecting to see Patsy Cline.

—Walt Miller, Nashville

You're worried about the neighborhood now that little Helen Bransford has married that New York writer.

—Kaul M. Williams, Nashville

You've ever lost your car at Starwood.

—Laura Ellis, Nashville

You are genuinely excited about the fact that a touring company of Phantom of the Opera will be at TPAC in two years.

—Susan Fanning, Nunnelly

You can sell your rock quarry for $10.5 million, get appointed to the Nashville Zoning Board, get the city to help you get a new quarry site, AND then sue the city if you don't get your way.

—Donna Silvey, Nashville

Your children think that everyone returns to the same spot on the interstate every year to watch the Fourth of July fireworks at Riverfront.

—Linda McFayden-Ketchum, Nashville

You have worked at WRLT-FM 100.
—*Robin Moore, Madison*

You buy an office building, tear it down, then can't raise money to build a new one.
—*Jeff Ockerman, Nashville*

You know about the naked would-be burglar at Pancake Pantry who strangled himself.
—*Annie Laurie Hardy, Nashville*

It is your hope and prayer that the Watson Pool Man will not wear shorts in his TV commercials this summer.
—*Kaul M. Williams, Nashville*

You have learned to multiply by 8.25 percent.
—*Barbi Taylor-Page, Nashville*

You've never crossed Charlotte.
—*John Denson, Nashville*

honorable mentions

You remember when Summer Lights was free—and profitable.

Jan Bell, Nashville

★

You still call it Candyland.

Laura Ellis, Nashville

★

You really don't trust women with short hair.

Lisa Abraham, Nashville

★

61

You think Animal Attractions is a new dating service.

—*Jerri L. Uhrig, Nashville*

Tour guides think that Johnny Cash once lived in your house, too.

—*Britt Lowry, Nashville*

You think "Go Big Orange" is foreplay.

—*Brian Davis, Antioch*

You attend church to secure a recording deal.

—*Steve Reynolds, Nashville*

You find yourself wondering if Shotgun Red is anatomically correct!

—*Carol Hudson, Smyrna*

You always "Do Lunch" wearing a tennis skirt but you don't play tennis.

—*Gina Carota, Nashville*

You give money to the symphony but never attend.

—*Lynn A. Thornton, Nashville*

You miss Jimmy Stahlman.

—*John Denson, Nashville*

You think *The Tennessean* and *Nashville Banner* still vie editorially.

—*John Denson, Nashville*

You've reached the point in your life that pinstripes go with glen plaid.

—*John Denson, Nashville*

The baby gift that you sent Garth and Sandy Brooks was handmade by you.

—*Kaul M. Williams, Nashville*

Your pickup truck's rear window is a White Way Cleaners bag and duct tape.

—*Mike Curley, Nashville*

You'd rather drop the schools than pay a state tax.

—*Steve Meigs, Nashville*

You cut back on your trips to Atlanta as soon as The Nature Company opened.

—*Pam Reese, Nashville*

You believe you are one of the select few on Bob Clement's mailing list.

—*Jim Pack, Nashville*

Rather than "yes," you scream "okey-dokey" during an orgasm.

—*Dana Jackson, Nashville*

You call a garden hose a hose pipe.

—*Harry E. McCormick, Nashville*

You wanna be seen at the Stock-Yard.

—*Richard Scott, White House*

"Booty" is a major word in your vocabulary.

—*Jim Chapman, Nashville*

You remember the gap between Dan McDaniel's front teeth.

—*Kaul M. Williams, Nashville*

You believe Barbara Mandrell loves prunes.

—*Herman Yeatman, Nashville*

You tell your beautician to do your hair "just like Demetria's."

—*Don Wirth, Nashville*

Selling plasma is always an option.

—*Lisa Abraham, Nashville*

You think that the Junior Chamber is a great place to meet the movers and the shakers.

—*Chip Alvey, Nashville*

honorable mentions

You go to the airport to see an art exhibit.

Ken Lass, Nashville

You think that a great performance at TPAC is your daughter's dance recital.

Mary Lou Edgar, Nashville

You've taken a leak in the sink at Starwood.

Syd Lovelace, Nashville

You've shushed someone at the Bluebird.

Suzy Ward, Nashville

You got a Pepsi Gotta Have It Card so you think your credit report must have improved.

—H.R. Carpenter, Nashville

You've spent a lot of time at Davis-Kidd looking for *Deep Thoughts* by Jack Handey.

—Cayce Clay, Nashville

You make an ice cream float with a diet drink.

—H. Polston, Nashville

You go to the Cooker, order just a tea, and tell the server to keep the rolls coming.

—Lisa Abraham, Nashville

You still think HCA is a good investment.

—Jan Bell, Nashville

You speak to pets but not pet owners.

—Lisa Abraham, Nashville

Your money is older that you are.

—Jan Bell, Nashville

Your BMW has a "People for Perot" bumper sticker.

—*Ken Lass, Nashville*

Your garbage man gets paid more than your kids' teachers.

—*Ted W. Davis III, Nashville*

You have always wondered what happened to the Shoney's Big Boy statues.

—*Todd Lester, Nashville*

You're starting to miss Fate Thomas' barbecue.

—*Syd Lovelace, Nashville*

You think Catholics really do worship statues.

—*Chip Alvey, Nashville*

You are looking forward to global warming so you can play in the lake all year round.

—*Terri Wood, Madison*

You cackle gleefully every time you see a truckload of wooden pallets.

—*Jay Hitt, Nashville*

You actually feel that you are surrounded by friends at Faison's.

—*Chip Alvey, Nashville*

You ask your female job applicants, "Are you pregnant yet, er what?"

—*Kathy Pennington, Nashville*

You believe that Dickerson Road was named for a sexual activity.

—*Lynn A. Thornton, Nashville*

You watch a news item on CNN, see it the next day in *USA Today*, and see it the day after that in the local papers.

—*Ted W. Davis III, Nashville*

You had to be there

YOU ARE SO NASHVILLE IF...

★ Todd got your ex-girlfriend pregnant.

★ Your Swan Ball at Cheek-wood used a Main Course from Vincent Price's Selections—of Swan stuffed with goose, which is in turn stuffed with duck, veal, and finally larks. (References: *The People's Almanac. The Book of Lists.* Wallechinsky, David, Wallace, Irving, *Vincent Price's 10 Favorite Dinner Guests from all History*, pp. 419-420.)

★ You can tell I am so Nashville if.

★ You've realized that adding 65, 40, and 24 never gives a positive answer.

★ You can count your ex-girlfriends on one hand and none of them are named Roz.

★ Images of translucent news-casters accompanied by bad Jamaican music appear on downtown office buildings.

★ You are in negotiations with Oliver Stone about making a movie of Snow Bird's assassination.

★ You hear the name "Perot" and immediately think fried chicken or burgers.

★ You haven't figured out that the blinker on your car is not an accessory that makes the steering wheel look like "Mr. Potato Head."

★ You need a "pep talk;" your friend needs someone to laugh at what he says. "You see it vice versa" because his joke sounded like a fairy tale.

★ Two beers, a hat, and boots make you do that thang.

★ You haven't put a "6" on the end of a word since 1974.

★ You don't know where Vultee Boulevard is, but you like to say it over and over.

You bitch about Nashville's lack of culture, coffee shops, and clubs, but you get furious when Jay McInerney comes to town.
—*Brenda Jenkins, Nashville*

You read the *Nashville Scene*'s personal ads and think "BiWF" means "bicycle with fenders."
—*Greg Denton, Murfreesboro*

You start humming "Rocky Top" every time you see a stack of pallets lying around.
—*Neal McBrayer, Nashville*

The Sweetest Entries

You are so Nashville if...

The beauty of her lights at night still takes your breath away.
—*Barbi Taylor-Page, Nashville*

You make out-of-state residents feel welcome instead of calling them Yankees.
—*Carole Ann Jarusinsky, Nashville*

You enjoy riding the trolley and hanging out on Music Row to meet tourists to tell them what a great city you think Nashville is.
—*Charles L. Sowells, Nashville*

You tell a complete stranger "hello."
—*Angela Taylor, Nashville*

You live it and love it!
—*Quinn Shives, Nashville*

One of your fondest memories is of the day the Krystal server accidentally gave you an extra Krystal burger and straw in your sack-to-go.
—*Rachelfrost Roberts, Nashville*

You know you're a Nashvillian if you're in the *Scene*; if you have a wiggle to your walk and a twang to your talk. You love your home and you hold it dear. That's why I'm in Tennessee and I love it here.
—*Dena Royanne Price, Hermitage*

When your state's one in a million, when a smile greets your day, and neighbors call hey.
—*Deborah Armstrong, Nashville*

You hope your boyfriend proposes to you at the Sunset Grill.

—*Tamara Rosini-Laney, Nashville*

You are glad that the mayor can't do anything for seven hours at a time.

—*Jay West, Nashville*

You think that TPAC stands for "Tennesseans Peeking At Culture."

—*Susan Cavender, Nashville*

Your sister's name is "Sister."

—*Pat and Susan Shepherd, Brentwood*

Your bank changes its name more often than its interest rates.

—*Josh Whitmer, Nashville*

You can either recite your family history back 10 generations or you can't count that high.

—*Kathryn Spann, Nashville*

honorable mentions

You can't figure out why funding for the arts needs to be increased when you know for sure there are already three Picture Frame Warehouses.

Bill Shockey, Brentwood

When they blew up the Jefferson Street Bridge, you had to relocate your in-laws.

Britt Lowry, Nashville

You think Schermerhorn is a ride at Opryland.

Susan Cavender, Nashville

1993

Nashville was getting down to business in 1993.
Hammers were flying. Agreements were being signed. Deals were being negotiated.

Maybe it was the economy. Or maybe it was all the new coffee-houses. Three of them were in operation, and, with the smell of latte in the air, all that caffine-fueled energy had to go some-where.

From Gaylord Entertainment came announcements of the reno-vation of the Ryman Auditorium, the construction of a new club on Second Avenue, and the search for a professional sports team to buy. Hard Rock Cafe officials announced plans to open one of their restaurants on Second Avenue. American Airlines said it might soon be flying direct to London. Hospital Corporation of America, meanwhile, announced a merger with the bigger—and decidedly more aggressive—Columbia Healthcare Corp.

Mayor Phil Bredesen, no slouch himself, announced plans for a $140 million arena at the corner of Fifth Avenue and Broadway.

He told Metro Council he also wanted to purchase 535 acres of land near Shelby Park for a riverfront greenway. And he told the school board to get moving on magnet schools—he wanted dozens of them, pronto.

Everywhere you looked, there was activity, some of it decidedly un-Nashville in character. The Chamber of Commerce, in a fit of progressivism, announced that Music City had outbid New York and San Diego to become the host of the 1994 Gay Softball World Series. When that news reached Metro Council, fireworks flew. Meanwhile, Gov. Ned McWherter, nearing the end of his term, announced plans to build I-880 North, a $500 million northern freeway loop around Nashville. He also announced a novel health care program to replace Medicaid, dubbing it TennCare.

A citizens' action group, Nashville's Agenda, began discussing a host of initiatives in health care, housing, and the arts, all with an eye toward improving the city's quality of life. Vanderbilt alums started searching for a new basketball coach because former roundballer Eddie Fogler, well-respected by all, had left for South Carolina. Dollar General built a store in the Sam Levy housing projects to help area residents learn job-training skills.

Meanwhile, politics was bubbling like hot redeye gravy. Bredesen, early in the year, told a classroom of sixth-graders that he liked his job so much he would not run for governor of Tennessee in 1994. But, as the race drew nearer, Bredesen changed his mind, opened his checkbook, and took his shot at the state's top office.

Amidst the sound and the fury, something else was growing too: concern about crime. At an automatic teller machine on Blakemore Avenue, a stone's throw from Hillsboro Village and Vanderbilt University, a teenager, Elysia Coughlan, was slain and robbed of $20. Three teenagers were arrested in the murder. The city mourned her death.

While keeping candlelight vigils, residents wondered where their city was going. The question being asked by many was: Is bigger necessarily better?

YOU ARE SO NASHVILLE IF...

1st Place

Your church congregation is referred to as "the studio audience."
—*Sharon Kasserman*

2nd Place

You took food to Twitty City after the funeral.

—Lynetta Alexander

3rd Place

You hear two people conversing in a foreign language and you wonder if they're terrorists.

—Ira Rogers

Municipal Auditorium meets all your entertainment needs.

—Tambi Swiney

You are female and your best friend is your mother.

—Kelly Christie

You've been to Paris and to Athens, you've seen the Mona Lisa and the Parthenon, and you've never left the state of Tennessee.

—Mary Skinner

You *really* care what your restaurant server's name is.

—Betty Frankenbach

You think Nashville is the center of the universe because it's halfway between Graceland and Pigeon Forge.

—Michael Morse and Sheila Lorenz

You gossip about the private lives of country music stars— and *whisper* when you do.

—T.E. Barnes

You think about Fate Thomas every time you smell barbecue.

—Bart Graves

You have heard Larry Schmittou speak and still cannot understand how he has failed "ta branguh majer ligg baishbawl bidnish ta Nieshfull."

—Richard Courtney

You've ever yelled at someone who was speeding at Radnor Lake.

—*Susan Gray*

You go through parking lots to avoid the long lines at the turn signals.

—*Keith J. Gustavson*

You applaud between movements at the Nashville Symphony and cough the rest of the time.

—*Mary Smythe*

You're hoping that, if they get a river shuttle service between Opryland and downtown, they'll allow fishing.

—*Bill Shockey*

It breaks your heart to see Paul Eels selling Craftmatic chairs on TV.

—*Bart Graves*

You believe that General and Meharry should merge with the *General Jackson* for Nashville's first-class hospital ship.

—*Lynn Scarborough*

honorable mentions

You wonder if the state will still provide nightly messages on the side of the American General building when they move in—and if so, will it be a full-time position?

Nancy Wellford House

You can conjugate "Kroger."

Diane Van Dyke

You joined St. George's Episcopal Church to get a promotion at work.

Mark Kooyman

★

You think Green Hills School of Dance ought to teach Gatoring.

—*Mary Shelton*

Your movie theater is a bookstore and your bookstore is a cafe.

—*Lory Montgomery*

Your governor is doing better at reforming health care than the President.

—*Andy Coulter*

You willingly pay an extra 50 cents a week for your morning newspaper subscription, entitling you to a weekly supplement containing actual news.

—*Mary Smythe*

You consider macaroni and cheese as a vegetable option at a meat-and-three.

—*Chris and Pam Panfil*

You exchange business cards over the breakfast bar at Shoney's.

—*Dan Mazer*

You think "bleu cheese" is a typo.

—*Judy Jacobs*

You organize a benefit at the Bluebird for Pepsi can tampering.

—*Bart Graves*

You think "Al Dente" plays shortstop for the Sounds.

—*Jennifer George*

You park your car on your lawn when the driveway is empty.

—*Gaida Malins*

You strongly opposed Clinton's energy tax because of its effect on the price of NASCAR tickets.

—*Andy Coulter*

You wave back at the school crossing guards.

—*The Moses Lab*

You move to Brentwood and open up a mother-in-law apartment in the trunk of your car.

—*Wilson Davis*

You're producing the bag boy at Kroger.

—*Dan Mazer*

You buy a house in Brentwood—but can't afford to buy furniture for it.

—*Tony Grimes*

The bag boy at Kroger is producing you.

—*Dan Mazer*

Larry Schmittou has given you a personal tour inside the new Sounds scoreboard.

—*Jim Clay*

You sell your tickets for the free Reba McEntire concert.

—*Susan Houston*

You think that table service at Burger King makes a difference.
—*Lisa L. Kennedy*

Demetria Kalodimos walks into your favorite restaurant and you call your mom to tell her who you just saw.
—*Robert Meyer*

You've ever folded the Land o' Lakes butter carton so the Indian princess looks like she's topless.
—*Steven Leasure*

You can't take another Ralph Emery departure.
—*Cayce Clay*

When applying for a real job, instead of admitting that you're in the music business, you tell them you have always longed to be a receptionist.
—*Debra Robertson*

You are so tired of seeing the outline of Eddie Fogler's head on the "You Greek-Me Greek" building.
—*Cayce Clay and Courtney Clay*

A six-pack of talls makes you do Phil Bredesen impressions.
—*Bart Graves*

You think Tandy Rice is a Japanese dessert.
—*Jamie Aulsebrook*

You know which Christ Church the Judds attend.
—*Donna Nolen*

You know that Christie of Christie Cookies is a guy.
—*Jan Bell*

You believe Jesus was a Protestant—more than likely, Church of Christ.
—*Robert Orr Jr.*

You find yourself driving past Granite Falls, just to see if you know anyone sitting on the patio—and honk your horn at them.

—*Tim Templeton*

Poison ivy makes you break out in "whelps."

—*Tania Owen*

You think Ralph Emery got a raw deal.

—*Denise Dunbar*

You paint your house any taupe-like color prior to selling it.

—*Tim Rauhuff*

You keep trying to figure out what Anne Brown knows about who.

—*Jan Bell*

You miss the old airport.

—*Sandra Johnson*

You use a co-writer to compile your grocery list.

—*Dennis A. Taylor*

You called Channel 8 to complain when Barney was taken off the air.

—*Tambi Swiney*

You can pronounce Bob Meade's name in Italian.

—*Rhee Bevere*

You stand up for Jesus and sit down to mow the lawn.

—*Ron Kidd*

You have absolutely no idea who Granny White was.

—*Frank Hart Smith*

You spend $100,000 for an application for an NBA franchise and your property receives a $2 million tax reduction.

—*Jimmy Mulcahy*

Ones We Can't Explain

YOU ARE SO NASHVILLE IF...

★ Your car has more power than your car.

★ You think "maitre d'" is a parrot.

★ You are not fat and all out of shape I am like the little girl was on a crowded bus too much fat people in here a fat world we are in these days if you are fat forgive I heard a preacher once say go take off close and stand in front of the mirror and take a good look at yourself Forgive me it's true.

★ Your son's sister is "doiter."

★ You attach a zip code to your stairway to heaven.

★ You like your rock in the ground, your roll in the hills, and your country in the air.

★ You're driving home from Florida with a friend who has Florida tags on her car, and another Florida car with a couple in it drives up and says "What city?" and you lean out of her car and say "Nashville!"

★ You take time to "smell the flowers" and sneeze!

★ You not only don't miss the *P.O.V.* series on WDCN— you've never even heard of it!

★ You go to the fishing rodeo and fight 20,000 fishing hooks to catch one fish, and don't catch a thing, until after it's over, and then you catch a stringer full (a prize in itself).

★ Given the choice between buying a new set of bass strings and buying new shoes for your kid, you steal the strings and buy a bag of pot.

★ Your evening prayer is: Lord, send that big hall for basketball, and a linedance partner who's deft, some new schools with "old" rules, and jeans that don't show off my cleft. Amen. (West End version)

You've thought about shooting the next person who tells you to "have a Jim Dandy Day."

—*Adam Dread*

You know that Paul Randall doesn't *really* find Gerry House that funny.

—*Robert Orr Jr.*

Your best pickup line is, "Let's go out to your car and listen to my new demo tape."

—*Rhee Bevere*

You think *The Firm* is Southern lit.

—*Kim Fennell*

You still believe that Beverly Briley had a driving disorder.

—*Susan Gray*

You'd rather have the T-shirt than the $250 cash.

—*Larry Grigsby*

You are sick and tired of Dan Walters commercials.
—*Paul Miller*

You actually call it "The District."
—*Adrienne Nash*

Your signal for the end of winter is the sudden appearance of Demetria Kalodimos' tan.
—*Santos B. Lopez*

You've got a great story about seeing one of the Hager twins really drunk, but you're not exactly sure which one it was.
—*Bart Graves*

You get a frequent-shopper discount from Dr. Pat Maxwell.
—*David Bohan*

You lost a shoe at Deja Vu.
—*Richard Scott*

You listen to your kids three minutes a day and listen to Rush Limbaugh for three hours.
—*Bart Graves*

You randomly see women wearing black pantyhose and white pumps.
—*Allison Migliore*

You plan your route to work in order to drive past the maximum number of Tanya Tucker billboards.

—Larry McKee

You think Belle Meade Brasserie is an upscale lingerie store.

—Bonnie Huettig

While on vacation, you tell someone you are from Nashville, and they ask, "How's Dolly Parton?" and you say, "Fine," even though you've never seen her.

—Kenny Mann

You think that ethnics are people who belong to any church other than yours.

—Ira Rogers

You know you should report your gay neighbors to someone.

—Cindy Moskovitz

The hope of what Nashville could be has kept you from moving somewhere else.

—Wilson Davis

You think The Steeplechase is a handy guide to the churches of Nashville.

—*Stephanie Marks-Ryan*

You've considered donating a spell-check program to *The Tennessean*.

—*Ron Kidd*

You absolutely could not, even under the threat of agonizing death, clap on the downbeat.

—*Walter Jowers*

You think the NES building is the State Capitol.

—*Shari Hopkins*

You still think the Wave Pool has AIDS.

—*Cindy Cates*

You strike a cool pose when you get on a mall escalator.

—*Ted Gray*

You approve of Christians playing softball but deny homosexuals the same right.

—*Tony Dorris*

You canceled your subscription to *Foreign Affairs* magazine to take the Saturday *Tennessean*.

—*Jim Clay*

You describe our neighborhoods as "Green Hills," "The Good Side" of Belmont, "The Bad Side" of Belmont, and "Across The River."

—*Trasbin Stoner*

"Church of Christ and Uncoordinated" is the excuse you give for not wanting to dance.

—*Ted Gray*

You want your daughter to go to a magnet school so she'll be like Dinah Shore.

—*Mary Shelton*

You just don't get most of the "You Are So Nashville If..." entries.

—*Cindy Moskovitz*

You wonder *who* decides which lights stay on and which are turned off in the American General Building.

—*Allison Migliore*

You are a little confused by the coffee menu at Bongo Java.

—*Candice Sanders*

You call those plastic forks "silverware."

—*Judy Jacobs*

You use your church bulletin for a 10 percent restaurant discount.

—*Betty Frankenbach*

You spend your lunch hour counting out-of-state cars going the wrong way on one-way streets.

—*Jessie Neahous*

You think "Judd Nelson" is a double bill.

—*Dave Hickey*

HUH?

NASHVILLE SCENE
YOU ARE SO NASHVILLE IF...

The Albies

No matter how much bitterness, resentment, and despair this contest exposes, we can always count on a few stray beams of sunshine from loyal readers. Their memories of Nashville are as vast as their goodwill. In honor of our unashamedly maudlin publisher, Albert J. Del Favero Jr.—who fondly remembers dates at the Belle Meade Theater, sandwiches at Moon Drugs, and those golden days when the Allman Joys played in his garage—we present the nice-guy entries... the Albies.

YOU ARE SO ALBIE IF...

★ You saw John F. Kennedy at Dudley Field.

★ You can remember that all of Al Gore's stories in *The Tennessean* were accompanied by photographs taken by Tipper.

★ You miss the steak & biscuits at Ireland's, the sodas and BLTs at Candyland, Shacklet's good cafeteria food, Cross Keys' hamburgers, Spinnakers' fresh bread in a flower pot, B&W's reasonable prices, malts at the Chocolate Shoppe, deep dish pizza at JD Doublecrust, Charlie Nickens' barbecue on corn cakes, the ambiance at the old Gerst House, cruising at Shoney's drive-in, cherry cokes at Brown's drugstore soda fountain, the pretty window front at Ruby Tuesday's on West End, sitting around Judy West's piano bar (something like *Cheers*) with your own personalized mug, the waitresses in shorts serving you in your car at Bar-B-Cutie, cracker ball soup at Kleman's on Union St., etc., etc.

* You describe a building block as a "Bricko Block." (Bricko refers to Breeko Block Mfg. Co., now gone.)

* You shopped at Harvey's or Cain-Sloan, had lunch at the "Monkey Bar," then snuck some Krystals into the Tennessee Theater and caught the bus home afterward.

* You regularly attended the Popeye Club at the Paramount Theater every Saturday— some years ago.

* You give directions around Nashville according to where things used to be—downtown Sears, Tennessee Theater, Harvey's, Zayre's, Genesco Shoe Commissary, etc, *ad consuetudinem*.

* You remember the beautiful Nativity scene at Centennial Park sponsored by Harvey's Department Store.

* You got your first kiss behind the concession stand at Cascade Plunge.

* You still go to Hutcherson's Pharmacy across from the David Lipscomb campus to get a *real* chocolate milkshake.

* You remember seeing Steve Martin fake an accident to stop traffic on Elliston Place after a show at the Exit/In.

* You remember hearing Francis Craig play "Near You" at the Hermitage Hotel.

Your driver's license has expired, but you get a new KDF Rock card every year.

—*Michael Morse and Sheila Lorenz*

You've given a pet name to the road kill you pass on the interstate every day.

—*Melissa Anne Sullivan*

You fought I-440 fiercely.

—*Robert Meyer*

You have more strip clubs than movie theaters.

—*Andy Coulter*

You fail to wonder why, in the reaction shots, the *Crook and Chase* audiences always appear to be on whoopee cushions.

—*Stacy Harrin*

You just don't understand most of the articles in the *Nashville Scene*.

—*Nancy Locke*

You think Nashville theater is alive and well as long as The Barn is open.

—*Sally Weatherford*

You only go to see the Sounds on Chicken Night.

—*Shari Hopkins*

You grew up on Hill's groceries but shop at Kroger now because it sells beer.

—*Candice Sanders*

You think TennCare is only for families of 10.

—*Dawn O'Kieff*

Paula of Rotier's has embarrassed you in front of your peers.

—*Lynn Scarborough*

You believe cable is an inalienable right.

—*Lisa L. Kennedy*

honorable mentions

You can name all the waiters at Jimmy Kelly's— and nobody on the Metro Council.

Bart Graves

You wish Tanya Tucker would stalk *you*.

Bart Graves

You always do better at Hill's.

John Petrucelli

You think that Joe Wyatt cares what Joe Biddle thinks.

Burton Augst

The Sweetest Entries

YOU ARE SO NASHVILLE IF...

★ You still have pride in Southern traditions.

★ You wake up each morning with a song in your heart!

★ You possess a high ethical character with an open mind and the IQ to see the light that reflects the sky is the limit to what Nashville can offer.

★ You agree with George Jones (he don't need no rocking chair).

★ You pack a picnic basket and go to the park to enjoy the Nashville Symphony.

★ You're a musician who was born in New York, lived years in L.A., and finally realized Nashville is the place to be!

★ An old country song still brings a tear to your eye.

★ You're nice to tourists not just because they add $1.7 billion to our coffers each year, but because that's the way you were "raised."

★ You think this is one of the coolest places to be living now.

★ While watching *Jeopardy* you give the question "What is Opryland" as the answer to "It is the eighth wonder of the world."

You supported Bredesen's new arena because you're tired of driving to Murfreesboro to see professional wrestling.

> —*Michael Morse and Sheila Lorenz*

You think Athena is the goddess of women's basketball.

> —*Polly Graves*

You once bet $100 you could tell a Krystal from a White Castle... blindfolded. And you won!

> —*Bart Graves*

The ashtrays in your house came from Bill Boner's yard sale.

> —*Chris Chamberlain*

You think the arena is more important than an education.

> —*Christy Sobel*

You think Billy Ray Cyrus should cut the *rest* of his hair.

> —*Lynn Sparkman*

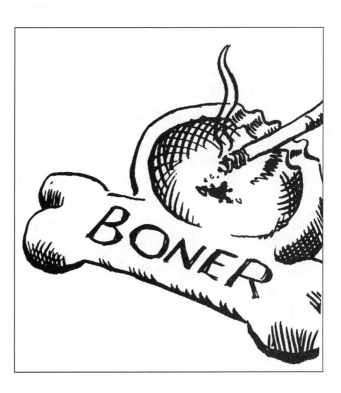

You aspire to line dance buck-naked.

—Lynn Sparkman

You believe every single word in the Bible is the truth and both historically and scientifically accurate. Except, of course, the word "wine" really means grape juice.

—Robert Orr Jr.

You wear your ankle bracelet *inside* your stockings.

—Sally Weatherford

Your favorite foreign film is Fuji.

—Lisa L. Kennedy

You kept asking, "Harlan who?"

—Jan Bell

You think foreplay is the Grand Ole Opry.

—Jeff Phillips

You spent too much time working on this.

—Ted Gray

You parallel park front end first.

—Ann Meador Shayne

You might could talk normal, but just cain't.

—Traci Cowles

You put an *S* on the end of Kroger, Amerigo, and Castner-Knott.

—Bart Graves

You've had a baby at Baptist—or made a commercial about being treated there.

—Fran Ross

Your insurance man talks like a preacher, and your preacher talks like an insurance man.

—Walter Jowers

You're very friendly and hospitable toward the person you're scalping tickets to.

—Andy Coulter

You drive through Krystal on your way home from Bread & Co.

—Ann Meador Shayne

honorable mention

You were expelled from Webb School for smoking.

David Kinnard

You're moving wherever the Sounds are!

—*Shawn Bilbrey*

You won't go to the super-market without makeup.

—*Tim Rauhuff*

Your church took a special collection for traffic cones.

—*Ron Kidd*

You think Van Gogh painted "Dogs Playing Poker."

—*Dave Hickey*

Your designated driver is drunker than you are at a Starwood concert.

—*Keith J. Gustavson*

Neither of your first two names gives an adequate clue to your gender.

—*Yvonne Martin Kidd*

You really do tell advertisers that Les Jameson sent you.

—*Stacy Harrin*

Your hair is so big that you're afraid to tease it.

—*Marshall Chapman*

Your policeman and your bookie are one and the same.

—*Rob Schmid*

1994

In hindsight, perhaps, the city could have blamed this year on El Niño. As it turned out, 1994 was not a year of rational expectations. It was a year of sudden bursts, cloudbreaks, surges, and surprises.

In November came the Republican Revolution, the Contract with America, and an amazing GOP landslide that ushered in Fred Thompson, Don Sundquist, and Bill Frist. Swept off the ballot were Democrats Jim Cooper, Jim Sasser, and our own mayor, Phil Bredesen, who aspired to be governor. Few had predicted it; fewer still were sure what the political revolution meant.

While the political developments were the work of humanity, nature also provided its own surprises. One February day, the mercury dropped, and an ice storm—the worst in 40 years—brought the city to its knees. Tree branches double-dipped, trunks snapped, and virtually all human activity ground to a halt. Thousands went without power for days, and hotels were packed. Without Bill Boner to kick around, the city had a new punching bag: Nashville Electric Service.

Other unexpected events dominated the headlines. Wynonna Judd announced she was pregnant by her boyfriend/non-husband, local boat salesman Arch Kelley. Soon, armchair moralists were bemoaning the further decline of their role models.

Columbia/HCA President Richard Scott told a Louisville civic group that his newly merged hospital company would keep its corporate headquarters in Louisville. Later, Scott and hometown HCA chief Tom Frist reversed their story: They were coming to Music City after all.

Politically, Nashville did the unexpected and elected a woman sheriff. Gayle Ray, who had no experience in law enforcement or corrections, defeated incumbent Hank Hillin. Soul singer La Toya Jackson came to Nashville to record an album. It was—surprise!—country. And at a commercial development site near Cool Springs, where everything is new and big and expensive, a 20,000-year-old mastodon tusk was unearthed.

Unfortunately, the year had its share of tragedy. Terrance Murray, a seventh grader at John Trotwood Moore, became the first student to be shot dead in a Metro public school. Among others, basketball player Michael Jordan sent condolences.

But there was good news too. The Bordeaux Landfill closed, and neighbors rejoiced. Country performers Travis Tritt, Clint Black, and Tanya Tucker played during halftime at the Super Bowl, giving further credence to the belief that country music was becoming the nation's musical art form. And interest rates fell, causing a massive spurt of home-buying in the city.

Finally, Pink Floyd came to town and played a concert in Vanderbilt's football stadium. The music was so loud that some area residents threw impromptu parties on their patios. Once again, the story had a surprise ending: Owing to the ruckus, there would never be a night-time concert in the stadium again.

YOU ARE SO NASHVILLE IF...

1st Place

You think that the H.O.V. lane is for people with AIDS.

—Paul Allen

honorable mentions

Your sister's name is "Sister."

Don Wirth

Your current mayor's 20-year-old divorce papers are big news.

Nancye Willis

You're not at all surprised to see Jell-O or macaroni and cheese on a list of vegetables.

Dana M. Lowe

Tonya Harding reminds you of your best friend in high school.

Nancye Willis

2nd Place

You live in Williamson County.

—Penny Phillips

3rd Place

Your legislator is trying to ban nudity because you don't have any place to conceal a weapon.

—Greg Denton

4th Place

You ever got out of doing something you didn't want to do by claiming it was a church night.

—Bryan Curtis

5th Place

You thought that Phil Bredesen *was* the governor.

—Marshall A. Osborne

You've ever announced to your waiter/waitress that you're a close personal friend of Jody Faison's.

—Kristin Gardner

You go to a Chinese restaurant, order hot tea, and add sugar.

—*Mickey Clark*

You think *The Morning Show* just isn't quite the same since Ralph Emery quit.

—*Don Wirth*

You refuse to go to Vanderbilt Hospital because you heard they experiment on people.

—*Bart Graves*

You root for U.T. instead of Vanderbilt because it's so much easier to spell "U.T."

—*Lee Levinson*

You're the 398th person to request "BUBBA" on your vanity plate.

—*Cindy Solomon*

You thought that you would get power the day after the ice storm because you go to church with somebody who works at NES.

—*Bill Shockey*

honorable mentions

You have to identify your fruits and vegetables to the Kroger checkout person.

Lary Frederiksen

You know John F. Lawhon is *not* going out of business.

Teri Frey

You're fretting about the 1996 presidential election because you're friends with both the Gores and the Alexanders.

Daniel Brabson

You find the thought of John Q. Bubba carrying a concealed weapon less alarming than a gay softball tournament.

—*Virginia A. McCoy*

You can remember when everyone you knew was from Nashville.

—*Carol Goff*

You secretly long for the days when Bill Boner and Fate Thomas ruled.

—*Don Wirth*

In conversations with others, you often find yourself thinking "Yep, s/he's going to hell."

—*Vic Pestrak*

You can remember the three different names of the same street you've been traveling on.

—*Joseph Carr*

You've never been to the Grand Ole Opry, the Hermitage, the Parthenon, the State Capitol, Cheekwood, Opryland, Cumberland Science Museum, Grassmere Wildlife Park, the Country Music Hall of Fame, or the Nashville Zoo.

—*Cindy Solomon*

Your child's scout troop is completing a badge in karaoke.

—*Kimberly Kimbrough*

You support the public school system but send your kids to a private school.

—*Cindy Solomon*

Your guitar has survived more marriages than your Cadillac.

—*Chuck Moan*

You try to get in touch with your Inner Bubba.

—*Bart Graves*

John J. Hooker reminds you of Minnie Pearl.

—*Richard Courtney*

Anyone from Fan Fair has asked, "Are you somebody?"

—*Heather Risley*

Demetria Kalodimos is a household name.

—*Laurie LaPointe*

Your sushi bar plays country music.

—*Roger Stenart*

You think that port-a-potties should be installed in the new arena to save money.

—*Brian Cullen*

The cattle stampede at the Wildhorse opening reminded you of the Shoney's breakfast bar.

—*Joe Walker*

You think The Olive Garden is an Italian restaurant.

—*Joe Dematteo*

The only things about the *XXX's and OOO's* pilot episode that even remotely seemed like the life you know in Nashville were the two scenes involving bad drivers.

—*Jeanette DeMain*

You go to the Nashville Symphony and hold up a Bic lighter at the end.

—*Bart Graves*

You wish Traci Peel would come back too.

—*Greg Denton*

You seriously considered mailing Matthew Cordaro the whole salmon that sat in your powerless freezer for a week.

—*Nancye Willis*

Your favorite announcer is the guy who does the voiceovers on the Emma's commercials.

—*Don Wirth*

You take your prom date to Grand Ole Golf after the dance.

—*Andy Collier*

You write country music but don't listen to it.

—*Diane Johnson*

Your reply to a panhandler is "I'm a musician," and he apologizes and walks off.

—*Perry Bolin*

You have more than two prescription antihistamines in your medicine cabinet.

—*Penny Phillips*

You ask for cornbread at a Chinese restaurant.

—*Jan Bell*

You're more concerned about the line at Bread & Co. than the bread line at the Mission.

—*Bill Shockey*

You think the statue behind the Ryman auditorium is Ned McWherter.

—*Greg Denton*

You think the Bicentennial Mall will be a great place to shop.

—*Jack Turner*

You see prisoners in orange coveralls and assume that they are big U.T. fans.

—*Colleen Mead*

As you were watching O.J. Simpson flee the Los Angeles police, you kept thinking, "That sure is a nice truck he's riding in."

—*Steven P. Gill*

You give Michael Jordan a standing ovation at a ball game, even if he doesn't get to play.

—*Lorrie Pope*

Your dog barks at the South Central Bell Tower.

—*Warwick Lawrie*

Your pastor used Wynonna's pregnancy to make a point during his sermon.

Bitsy Weaver

★

You thought "Crook" and "Chase" were terms that described most of our political races.

—Cayce Clay

You keep wondering why the Formosa family opened up a Chinese restaurant on 21st Avenue.

—Emily Shacklett

It's April and you're still driving a truck with a Christmas wreath wired to the grill.

—Danny Ayala

You liked the Swine Ball better when it was under the bridge.

—Nancye Willis

You're upset that the Corps of Engineers wants to charge you a couple of bucks to launch your $10,000 boat.

—Greg Denton

You understand perfectly when a customer at Bro's Cajun Cuisine asks, "What's the difference between Cajun and Creole?" and the waitress replies, "I don't know—I'm from Green Hills."

—David L. Ward

You think Sinking Creek is in Antioch and overflows every spring.

—Jan Bell

You've changed churches so you can still stop at Krispy Kreme on the way.

—Gavin Matlock

You thought Gayle Ray would look *sooo* cute in a police skirt.

—Gavin Matlock

Your 15 minutes of fame came while you were a phone-bank bid taker at Action Auction.

—R.M. McAlister

You practice for your Tennessee driver's license test at the video arcade.

—*D.L. Nelms*

You had a seat on the first flight to London.

—*Paula Flicker*

You have considered offering an NES lineman sex in exchange for power.

—*C. Goddard*

You believe the taxi will be there in 15 minutes like the dispatcher says.

—*Jack G. Simpson Jr.*

The biggest question in your mind about the mysterious Bredesen-divorce fax is, "How do you delete the phone number from the fax machine?"

—*Nancye Willis*

You think the painted lines on downtown sidewalks are there to help state employees find their way back to work after lunch.

—*Greg Denton*

You think *The Lion King* is about all the fibs Elvis told.

—*Brian Cullen*

Ones We Can't Explain

★ You think a bottle of soda is a bottle of Arm & Hammer rather than Pepsi or Coke (or commonly known as cold drink).

★ You have a pool table in your front yard. (There is actually one in front of a trailer on Charlotte Avenue.)

★ You know five or six certifiably bizarre local individuals, and you run into every one of them the first night your family is in town.

★ Giving directions to Battery Lane—from Hillsboro Road go Harding Place East. From Franklin Road go Harding Place West.

★ You're a state employee and carry a Kroger bag or Wal-Mart bag downtown.

★ Jimmy Davy called you at home (in the trailer park), mentioned your name in a column (twice), and invited you to see a baseball game when Nashville gets a major league team (Frank Vila to pitch).

★ An ordinary sedan turns your head, not a limo!

★ Your preacher wears a cowboy hat and boots while doing the two-step back and forth across the stage and yells hallelujah!

★ God is bread, but good is dead.

* You decide to cover your bald spot by following the examples of State Senator Thelma Harper and *Tennessean* columnist Catherine Darnell and getting the ugliest hat you can find surgically sewn to your head.

* You are seen playing air drums and (esp. cymbals) while driving or air drumming while driving.

* You go to films and Fuddrucker's with a co-writer of "Seven Spanish Angels" and eat at Gatti's with a former Vanderbilt basketball player.

* You think Charlotte Pike and Trinity Lane are the real names of Naomi Judd.

* You got so hot this summer that TennCare started to make sense.

* You visit Belle Meade Cafeteria, pay with exact change from your vinyl bag orange squeegie wallet, and hold up the line while you hunt for another penny, oblivious to the line forming behind you.

* You see Garth Brooks at FoodMax, and your cousins in Pelahatchie, Miss., scream at you cuz you didn't talk to him. Let the man buy milk for his babies.

* You're glad that Nashville has gotten its Boner back and wish that John Bobbitt could be so lucky.

You wonder whether Anne Holt and Jimmy Holt are related.

—*Stacy Harris*

You think Passover is a game show.

—*Mel and Kelly Watts*

Haji's named a roll after you.

—*Amy Adams*

You think Bill Clinton is a horrible president—but Al Gore is doing a wonderful job.

—*Andy Collier*

You can tell your out-of-town friends which part of the Centennial Park duck pond is the gay pick-up area.

—*Danny Ayala*

You still hate Eddie Fogler.

—*Jan Bell*

You think Sfuzzi's Mona Lisa is just a really bad picture of Crystal Gayle.

—*Rich Maradik*

You were "just sick" about Michael English but "just so happy" for Wynonna.

—*Kathleen Gallagher Kemper*

You're not sure who is more dangerous: Mel Perry or the goddess Athena.

—*John Caldwell*

Your ex-secretary hit platinum.

—*Amy Adams*

You think of Judd Collins and Walter Cronkite in much the same way.

—*Dana M. Lowe*

You go to yet another Civil War reenactment hoping maybe this time it will end differently.

—*Frank Karchefski*

Your idea of a vegetarian meal is a vegetable plate at Sylvan Park.

—*Jim Vickers*

You think espresso is an overnight delivery service.

—*Dennis A. Taylor*

You feel a little bit guilty about doing your Christmas shopping at the Wildhorse gift shop this year instead of at Barbara Mandrell's.

—*Tamara Rosini-Laney*

The Sweetest Entries

YOU ARE SO NASHVILLE IF...

You can recall enjoying driving Franklin Pike in Oak Hill at 45 mph without tailgating and speeding.

—Ernie Blankenship

You can remember when John Tesh and Pat Sajak did the weekend news and weather at Channel 4.

—Lee Levinson

You water the "yard" (lawn) with the "hose pipe" (garden hose).

—Julie Wright

You still think that Bob Lobertini was easily our best TV weather person.

—Robert Stutts

You think Mr. Wentworth Caldwell just made the biggest marketing mistake of the decade.

—Laura Harris

You wake up with Gerry House every morning, have lunch at the Oldies Cafe with Kevin Conners every day, and fall asleep with J.J. Austin every night in Nashville After Dark.

—Cynthia Hollis

You call the Dulcimer Splash (Opryland) the Floom Zoom, or (2) You call the Rockin' Rollercoaster (Opryland) the Timbertopper, or (3) You give directions to Green Hills Wallpaper Warehouse by saying it's "Across from Cain-Sloan's in Green Hills."

—Eve Sarrett

You get a craving for barbecue after midnight and the only place you will go is Mary's.

—*Derek W. Elliott*

You eat at Cracker Barrel every Friday night for 10 years and never go back when they raise the blackberry cobbler price.

—*Wanda Denny*

You were around for the ice storm of '51 (The Big One) and the ice storm of '94 (The Irritating One).

—*Nancye Willis*

You know that the Belle Meade Buffet accepts checks but not plastic.

—*Liane E. Proctor*

Your relatives come in town and you take them to Music Row and you have a good time.

—*Craig Dore*

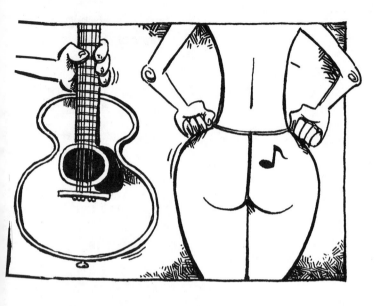

Your hairdo doesn't fit in your driver's license picture.

—*Leah Keys*

When planning a new municipal building, you spend more time contemplating its name than you do calculating its cost.

—*Penny Phillips*

You wonder why dance club performers will be required to wear G-strings—and what they'll do with the leftover E's, A's, D's, and B's.

—*Greg Denton*

You think the Parthenon is crumbling because it is, after all, thousands of years old.

—*John Caldwell*

You followed the cows being herded up Second Avenue and actually thought you made better time than usual.

—*Greg Denton*

Your mayor thinks you're smart enough to vote for him for governor, but too stupid to understand how to build an arena.

—*Nancye Willis*

You keep a personal mug at Bongo Java.
—*Amy Adams*

You begin all your business transactions by asking, "What years were *you* at MBA?"
—*Cindy Brooks*

You'd give more to PBS to show less.
—*Terry D. Robertson*

Your favorite deli is also your favorite gas station.
—*Doug Seroff*

You're on a first-name basis with the guy who stocks the hair spray at Kroger.
—*Kristi Seehafer*

You can name the entire Rotier family by name.
—*Maryglenn McCombs*

You wondered why Dewey Lineberry always insisted that the two of you have sex with the lights on.
—*Stacy Harris*

honorable mentions

You're upset about the amount of noise made at the Pink Floyd concert and want Vanderbilt to go back to having events where there is nothing to clap or cheer about—like Vanderbilt football games.

Greg Denton

★

Your Jiffy Lube has a Rush Room.

Bart Graves

★

You're from L.A.

Nan Allison

★

You bought season tickets for the Sounds because you thought that Michael Jordan would make the team.

—*Shannon Hardin*

You don't want a window seat on that airline flight because you don't want to mess up your hair.

—*R.M. Mead*

You're certain no one in your life is gay.

—*Douglas Fontaine*

The mariachi band at your local Mexican restaurant serenades you with "Rocky Top."

—*Nancye Willis*

You think that things have been going downhill ever since Bar-B-Cutie moved way out on Nolensville Road.

—*Don Wirth*

At some point in your Nashville education you went to school in a trailer.

—*David Hill*

Your idea of a big-city nightmare is paying $3 to park your car in a five-story garage.

—*Stan Hamilton*

You display your complete, autographed collection of H. Jackson Brown Jr.'s instruction books on your coffee table.

—*Anonymous*

You had your surgery performed at Baptist because of Barbara and Garth.

—*R.M. McAlister*

You have been miraculously cured of an incurable disease and your daughter is pregnant by immaculate conception.

—*R.M. McAlister*

You can't get an appointment with your doctor or lawyer because he's out campaigning for political office.

—*Sylvia Byrn*

You've ever thought about marrying Lorrie Morgan just to get a new pickup truck.

—*Bryan Curtis*

You think of Beano as an aperitif.

—*Nancye Willis*

You think Bart Graves is spending too much time on this.

—*Gordie Stewart*

You think Hooters will add to the ambiance of historic Second Avenue.

—*Tambi Swiney*

You're so intellectual that you read the *Nashville Scene* even when you *don't* have to go to the bathroom.

—*Greg Denton*

More We Can't Explain

★ You call Channel 5 to complain about Lelan's reference to the "Perspiration Indication," and the news director doesn't know what is wrong with that pronunciation—and says so.

★ You line dance to the theme song of *Hawaii Five-0*.

★ Your Domino's delivery car has windows.

★ You've got that look on your face. ("I'm a star!")

★ You've mistaken the South Central Bell building for a mutant cockroach attacking downtown.

★ Mamas, you want your babies to grow up and invest in the Nashville arena with money earned from working at the Chaos.

★ You can paint your office yellow in Brentwood.

★ You're obese, your husband has a potbelly, and your children are well on their way to being the same way!

★ Somewhere along your rise up the music industry ladder you've pampered Pepper.

★ You've finally realized, when lost, that if you just keep driving you'll get there.

You don't trust the winter weather report unless you get it from a puppet.

—*Adam Dread*

You think Slim Fast is a new country singer.

—*Brian Cullen*

You think TennCare is Hank Hillin's code name.

—*Stacy Harris*

Your mayor can afford to pay for a new $140 million arena out of his own pocket.

—*R.M. McAlister*

You go to Rivergate Toyota and ask for Dan Walters.

—*Nancye Willis*

Your child's back-to-school supplies include a bullet-proof vest.

—*Lory Montgomery*

You were shocked to discover the Gayle Ray you voted for was a woman.

—*Ken Lass*

While filling out this ballot, someone advises you to get a life.

—*Bart Graves*

You think red means "Six More Cars."

—*Ted Fontaine*

You see Drue Smith in Kroger and realize that she actually *chooses* to look that way.

—*Bill Ross*

1995

In 1995 Nashvillians were getting their first glimpse of Bud Adams. He was big. He was rich. He had a football team in Houston and he wanted to move it here.

Negotiations would go up and down for many months. As the secret talks went on, things started looking bright for Nashville football fans. Back in Houston, meanwhile, when a rally was held the week before Christmas to keep the Oilers from leaving their hometown, only 65 people showed up.

If the Oilers were keeping Nashville on the edge of collective hysteria, other sports news was breaking all around us. This was the year when an arena football league team was announced for Nashville, and a hockey team from New Jersey looked us over, too. But some of the biggest news of the year had nothing to do with sports. It had to do with killer tornadoes.

A strip mall in the Rivergate area was hit by a twister that overturned cars, ripped roofs off buildings, and sent shoppers fleeing for their lives. The same day, some 50 other tornadoes swept across Tennessee.

A tornado didn't strike country singer Ty Herndon, but for several weeks it looked like his career was wrecked. Having just recorded a No. 1 country tune, Herndon was arrested by a Dallas undercover policeman who was posing as a male prostitute. Eventually, Ty would survive the public relations nightmare. Meanwhile, there were happier times out at Opryland when George and Barbara Bush decided to spend their 50th wedding anniversary listening to some toe-tapping country music songs.

Columbia/HCA ended months of speculation when it announced plans to be based in Nashville. Reba McEntire announced a huge new structure on Music Row for her Starstruck Entertainment Complex. Unfortunately, she had to scrap plans for a heliport, which met intense public opposition.

Don Sundquist was inaugurated governor of Tennessee and almost immediately complained that Vice President Al Gore—and not he—had been named honorary chairman of the Tennessee Bicentennial Committee.

Meanwhile, the crap was also flying at Vanderbilt University, where some 500,000 starlings decided to roost, resulting in more natural fertilizer than the institution ever could have asked for. Sonic-boom shells were detonated to drive the birds away.

In one of the most unfortunate incidents of the year, two black churches and a black-owned tavern in Maury County were fire-bombed. It was part of a string of incidents that included burning crosses on church property and throwing beer bottles filled with gasoline.

There were plenty of disappointments in 1995. American Airlines canceled its Nashville-to-London flight. Henry Foster, former acting president of Meharry Medical College, was voted down as surgeon general nominee. Jimmy Bowen departed Liberty Records, where he had made Garth Brooks as household word.

But several other individuals moved on to greener pastures in 1995. Jim Sasser, the former U.S. senator, was named U.S. ambassador to China. And former sheriff Fate Thomas, released from prison, returned home and breathed new life into the Sureshot Rabbit Hunters Association dinner. Rabbit had never tasted so good.

This year the Committee of Insiders did not name a winner. Simply put, the committee did not find the entries to be that good.

As was noted in the Scene's *July 27, 1995, issue, "We didn't find the dozens of entries that, either for reasons of wit or judgment or point of view or insight or sheer creativity, could grace us with a moment of joy, a spark of self-recognition."*

We asked our readers "to respect us for making this difficult decision." We asked them to try harder the next year.

YOU ARE SO NASHVILLE IF...

You think that getting the Devils here fulfills a prophecy in Revelations.

—*Laurence Ralston*

You think every city has its art museum in an airport.

—*Wayne Mehl*

You repeatedly find yourself asking the Kroger produce boy where the Granny White apples are.

—*Leslie Dorn*

Your hospital provides doughnuts after blood cholesterol screenings.

—*Jan Liff and Nan Allison*

You voted for Fermo DePasquo but against beer in the arena.

—*Adam Dread*

You go to Deja Vu and ask, "So, where are the ugly ones?"
—*Julie Stagner*

You know Jesus' last name is Christ.
—*Stacy Harris*

You remember Dan Miller—but you can't remember why.
—*Stacy Harris*

You can't pro-nounce that Massey woman's first name.
—*Stacy Harris*

You think TPAC is a breath mint.
—*Eric Whistler*

Your church used to be Twitty City.
—*Paul and Susie Carmichael*

You blindfold yourself before letting people into your home.
—*Robert Meyer*

You think GOP stands for Grand Ole Opry.
—*Shanna Black*

All the broken-down cars in your front yard are jacked up on Bicentennial Mall bricks.

Adam Dread

★

Your senator is a cat killer and your governor is a dog thief.

Hank Fincher

★

You know whose Converse high-tops are hanging over Belmont Boulevard.

Mary Boyd and Louise Zepp

★

Your doctor wants to be your senator, your preacher wants to be your mayor, and your mayor wants to be your governor.

—*Bart Graves*

You head for the nearest mall when you hear there's a tornado coming.

—*Adam Dread*

You survived your shopping trip to Rivergate during the recent tornado—and asked for a rain check.

—*Dianne Gregory*

Your church gets its communion crackers from the kosher aisle at Kroger.

—*Hank Fincher*

You go to an Italian opera sung in English.

—*Kevin Haymes*

You name the new arena "The Nashville Arena."

—*Ann Roebuck*

Your river water has an octane rating.

—Chuck Hargrove

You cheer for both Vanderbilt and U.T. but you bet on Alabama.

—Kathleen Gallagher Kemper

You go to your favorite seafood restaurant and the person behind the counter asks, "Do you want that with cheese?"

—P.J. Donaldson Jr.

You can't let yourself get too attached to Dan Miller, because you know he'll leave again.

—Cayce Clay

Words are inadequate to express your appreciation to country stars who donate their time to appear in Baptist Hospital's TV commercials.

—Stacy Harris

Your dog is missing and you find him living at the Governor's Mansion.

—Shirley Peek

Your downtown arena looks like a toilet seat.

—Michael and Caroline Beroth

You went to Rivergate after the tornadoes hoping to find a good scratch and dent sale.

—Julie Stagner

You think Hope Hines looks suspiciously like John Doe #2.

—Bart Graves

You think beer sales should be prohibited within 100 feet of Al Gore.

—Lynn Niedermeier

You look forward to The Home Town Tour.

—Pam Orlando

You can't wait to see Dan Miller read the news while dressed in his bunny suit.

—Stacy Harris

You have wanted to have Rush Limbaugh perform at your child's birthday party.

—Philip R. Cloutier

You pray they won't serve beer, but you hope for the Devils to come here.

—Randy Gibson

You show up at Greer Stadium to see the Nashville Knights play.

—Dianne Gregory

You flunked the DNA test.

—Luther Beckett

You think Mosko's is a city in Russia.

—Farris Smith

Your local sports celebrities have names like Melissa, Tiffany, and Misty instead of Crusher, Mad Dog, and Killer.

—Jonathan F. Phillips

You went to see the Nashville Sounds play hockey at the Municipal Auditorium.

—Dianne Gregory

You listen to 103.3 KDF and really think you are on the cuttin' edge.

—Barry D. Cox

Your favorite song is "Beat It," your favorite movie is *Indecent Exposure*, and your favorite singer is Ty Herndon.

—Bill Bailey

You call Thunder 94 and Lightning 100 to complain about the reception in your car.

—Adam Dread

You know the only way you are going to get reserved seats at Starwood is to buy scalped tickets.

—*John Hutchings*

You have been diagnosed as having a case of Cellular Elbow.

—*Gary Delaney*

You hoped that they wouldn't allow beer in the new arena because you assumed that means they would allow "totally nude" table dancing.

—*Adam Dread*

Your incumbent mayor's strongest opponent lives in a van behind Shoney's.

—*Hank Fincher*

You were so proud to see that you lived in the nation's friendliest city, according to NBC's *Dateline*, then someone flipped you off on the way to work the next morning.

—*Joseph C. Estes Jr.*

NES does your landscaping.

Eric Whistler

★

You build a sports arena and the city fathers pass an ordinance prohibiting the selling of alcoholic beverages there.

—*Farris Smith*

You get married at the courthouse and then you take your bride down to Hooters for some Hot Wings!

—*Molly Ray*

Your private airport has complimentary Aquanet aerosol hairspray in the ladies' room.

—*Jennifer Corbitt*

You'll spend $20 million for a hockey team, but you think a "hat trick" is something a magician does with a rabbit.

—*Hank Fincher*

You wonder what kind of bait you use to catch gefilte fish.

—*Hank Fincher*

You stop at the gas station to buy beer more often than you stop there to buy gas.

—*Mark Gregory*

Your mayor likes beer with his hockey.

—*Jason Matson*

You think the word "spatial" means what you eat for lunch at Shoney's.

—*Duncan Currey III*

Every major network affiliate station says on the Saturday night weather broadcast at some point, "And for church time tomorrow..."

—*Joseph C. Estes Jr.*

You call it "the wine auction" because you can't pronounce "Un Eté du Vin" with a Southern accent.

—*Kathleen Gallagher Kemper*

You knew someone who was at Rivergate Mall when the tornado hit.

—*Joseph C. Estes Jr.*

You will pay $120 million to have a beer five feet from a church!

—*M. Grafton Smith*

You don't want your name in lights along Broadway.

—*Sherwood MacRae*

You can name three players from the New Jersey Devils.

—*Eric Whistler*

You learned most of the NHL rules this year.

—*Eric Whistler*

You actually attended the highly celebrated opening for the new Krispy Kreme.

—*Bob Riedel*

You wait on tables at Shoney's and have a record deal.

—*Alan Shipston*

In keeping with your New Year's resolution to get in shape, you join the Green Hills YMCA because they offer valet parking.

—*Andy Swallow*

You believe everything that Catherine Darnell says is true.

—*Junior Kimes*

The manager of your local grocery store has proudly posted a sign on the front of the store advertising "Mixed Bokays" in the floral department.

—*Suzanne M. Britt*

You remember "the good ole days" when a trip down Second Avenue meant you were lost.

—*Michael Hurst*

honorable mentions

You hung up on the Fantasy Man because you thought he was a telemarketer.

Hank Fincher

You think Pret a Porter is a portable toilet.

Soraya Kashani

You still fly American to support the hub.

Michael Smith

You think "Gaylord" is an alternative savior.

Carol A. Foutz

You take out-of-town guests to Cowboys LaCage to see Ty Herndon do his Wynonna impersonation!

—*Chuck Hargett*

You keep saying to yourself: He's from Dallas! Thank God Ty Herndon's from Dallas!

—*Chuck Hargett*

Your 100-foot tape measure only measures 85 feet.

—*David Shephard*

You think Kato is a babe.

—*Beth Rich*

You move here from L.A. or N.Y. to escape crime, pollution, and earthquakes—then whine about the city's lack of a real N.Y. deli, Spago's or Saks.

—*Janell Glasgow-Hall*

You go to the Southern Women's Show for the free food.

—*Beth Rich*

You go out to eat dinner and find the governor's next dog!
—*Steve Midgett*

You keep your umbrella on the gun rack in your pickup truck.
—*Coley Karr*

You think that Cowboys LaCage is a gay bar.
—*Susan Gennoe*

You remember when Dan Miller's weatherman was Pat Sajak.
—*Rachel Cotham*

You think Temple Hills is a Jewish country club.
—*Chuck Hargrove*

You hide your wine bottles under your newspaper in the curbside recycle bin so your Baptist neighbors won't talk.
—*Molly Malone*

You never understood why we had a direct flight to London, Ky., to begin with.
—*Jerry McCaskill*

On a job application, where it says "in case of emergency notify," you put 911.
—*Chuck Hargrove*

You think the privacy tarp around the Vanderbilt practice field really makes a difference.
—*John Wilhoite*

You think the CK on your designer shirt stands for Castner-Knott.
—*Barbara Hart*

You are so excited because you were able to book a room at the Murfreesboro Holiday Inn for the 1996 summer Olympics in Atlanta.
—*Cayce Clay*

You are accused of being called a moron, and you reply: No, I am a born-again.

—*P.J. Donaldson Jr.*

You have to travel to Knoxville to watch *Meet the Press*.

—*P.J. Donaldson Jr.*

On the morning of your wedding day you go to yard sales.

—*O.J. Giambattista*

You can buy cowboy boots at your favorite bar.

—*Jay McDowell*

You have to stop and rest more than once going into the Steeplechase because your beer cooler is too heavy.

—*Fant Smith*

You think hockey is a term which describes how you clear your throat.

—*Philip R. Cloutier*

Instead of getting angry at rude motorists, you pray for them.

—*Philip R. Cloutier*

You wonder why Metro Council could fund the cost of the new arena when it couldn't fund the cost of the alien landing pad.

—*Jim Clay*

You don't feel guilty about dropping off a box of stray puppies in front of the Governor's Mansion.

—Cayce Clay

When you call your agent, the person on the phone answers "Mama, it's for you."

—Sam Vester

You think the Classic Cat is where Garfield and Heathcliff live.

—Julie Stagner

Someone says "Bordeaux" and your first thought has nothing to do with fine wines.

—Emily Wrens

Your idea of a romantic interlude is having sex in a parked car on the shoulder of the interstate.

—Stacey McClendon

The local ballet company gives away free tickets and they still can't fill Polk Auditorium.

—Laura d'Angelo Loosen

Your "15 minutes of fame" occurred when you were seen at the Wildhorse on TNN.

—Mari Roberson

Dog dipping and hard rocking can coexist.

—Roger Black

You think the Exit/In is a sleazy motel.

—Dan Crass

You actually call Rivergate Toyota to see if Dan Walters was hurt in the recent tornado.

—Cayce Clay

Your mayor lost a fight with some chick named Peaches.

—Marie Patrick

You'll open your door, take off your clothes, and lay down blindfolded on a phone call from a man who says he'll fulfill your fantasy.

—*Connie Kay*

You think you know good art because you wear a Myles Maillie T-shirt.

—*Molly Malone*

When people ask you for ID, you say: 'Bout what?

—*Tom Caparelli*

You order cappuccino to chase your cornbread down.

—*Lavonia Arnold*

You're 85 feet away.

—*Jefferey Copeland*

You think the *Scene* is a radical newspaper.

—*Laurence Ralston*

You think the best line to use to pick up women is "Get in the truck, bitch."

—*Bill Seifert*

You're ready to push, pull, or drag Dan Walters through the streets of Rivergate.

—*Regina Sensing*

Your company advertises its business hours on Sunday as open after church.

—*Maureen Farley*

You thought the Bellevue Mall had already folded.

—*Kay Smith*

You think the Hermitage is the former home of *Alan* Jackson.

—*Tom Fedora*

Your mother has ever caused a fight in a bar.

—*Julie Stagner*

You've ever broken a fingernail trying to pick up the 7-10 split.

—*Julie Stagner*

You've wondered if the new Bicentennial Mall will have a Sears, some movie theaters, or a Pier 1.

—*Stan Schklar*

You think by showing your church bulletin you'll get discounts on beer at the new arena.

—*Paul T. Jack Sr.*

You thought Johnny Jackson's Soul Satisfaction was a weekly tent revival.

—*Brian F. Williams*

You think the proposed anti-immigration legislation would stop all those Californians from moving here.

—*Bobby Braddock*

You've ever shown friends a country music video and said, "See, there's my hand."

—*Robin Lawrence*

You can remember when Second Avenue was a lot less like Antioch.

—*Shannon Hardin*

You think "DiNardo" is Spanish for money.

—*Stacy Harris*

You believe the *Nashville Banner* has its priorities in order since it puts biblical quotations where they belong—on the op/ed page.

—*Stacy Harris*

You miss the commercials co-starring Dan Walters' wife and wonder why Dan's now introducing viewers to his "gal pal."

—*Stacy Harris*

You like the idea of calling our city's leader the Honorable Reverend-Mayor.

—*Leigh R. Hendry*

Your Daisy Dukes are short enough to expose your achy breaky heart.

—*Paul T. Jack Sr.*

You think that Catherine Darnell is a journalist.

—*Charles C. Holt*

It takes a Metro Council vote for your church to have wine during communion services.

—*Jamie W. Bird*

Before placing a lost-and-found ad to find your pet, you check the Governor's Mansion first.

—*Robert Meyer*

You come by car and leave by Greyhound.

—*Terry Chenault*

You've submitted a candidate for a Sunshine Award.

—*Pam Orlando*

You refer to the streets as "a solid sheet of ice" any time it snows.

—*Pam Orlando*

You're a Metro teacher with a child in private schools.

—*Cindi Thomas*

You think the phrase "boldly go where no one has gone before" is an advertising slogan for Fountain Square.

—*Glenn Stein*

You think it makes sense that the Nashville Zoo is in Clarksville.

—*Anonymous*

You've ever laughed when someone says, "Stay on Old Hickory Blvd. and you won't get lost."

—*Anonymous*

You see a crown-shaped air freshener in the back of someone's car and think it means they're British.

—*Laura Sebastian*

Your downtown historic district's oldest place of business is a three-year-old restaurant.

—*Anonymous*

You think every black musician you see is one of the Wooten Brothers.

—*Travis Corder*

You use a cellular phone at Kmart to call someone about a blue-light special.

—*Robin Lawrence*

You wish you'd come up with that "Fantasy Man" idea first.

Adam Dread

You're tired of this game.

—*Vanessa Wynn*

You have your glossy, autographed 8-by-10 framed on the wall of Acklen post office.

—*Vicky Bailey*

Your hair is longer than your wife's.

—*Tim Koch*

Your church has a time-and-temperature tower, and you think selling beer at the arena is tacky.

—*Ron Kidd*

You think Naomi Judd is too weak and sick to handle another round on the talk-show circuit.

—*Laura Sebastian*

You have the same ad running in the *Scene* personals and *Musicians Wanted*.

—*Robin Lawrence*

Thank you. Thank you very much

141

In the frozen pasturelands of Iowa and the snowy streets of New Hampshire, a sight familiar to Tennesseans was emerging: a flannel shirt with red-and black-checkered squares. The man wearing it was Lamar Alexander. He was running for president, and while he came close, there were no cigars. Bob Dole beat him like a drum.

Another local figure just as well known to Nashvillians was also making a run at another elective office. In the hidden alleys and broken sidewalks of East Nashville where he grew up, Bill Boner was seeking election to the state legislature. Against all odds, and dragging enough personal baggage to fill a dumptruck, he emerged victorious. Boner was back!

No political drama, however, gripped the city more than the tale that was emerging from a hillside in an upscale West Nashville neighborhood. There, police were scouring every square inch of land owned by Nashville attorney Perry March and his wife, Janet Levine March, who disappeared one August night. Police fingered Perry

March as the prime suspect in Janet's death or disappearance, but charges would never be filed.

From across the state came disturbing news of an epidemic of burnings of black churches. Gov. Don Sundquist appointed an 81-member task force to investigate the situation. National news reporters descended upon West Tennessee, where many of the burnings had taken place.

The pollution of the Cumberland River was a prime topic of conversation among city leaders. Vic Scoggin swam the entire length of the Cumberland and emerged on dry land in Kentucky to say that, over the 696 miles of his route, he had paddled through unbelievable filth, sewage, and scum. Meanwhile, red-faced officials from Metro Water Services acknowledged that they were forced to dump 35 million gallons of raw sewage into the river every day while they cleaned the water system's pipes.

As the city's public schools were drawn into a huge discussion about how to end busing, a private school became the focus of countless news stories. At the Phoenix Academy, headmistress and founder Barbara Bachman was charged with pilfering $300,000 from the new institution's coffers. Ultimately, the school was forced to close its doors.

Nashville lost two fine musicians in 1996. Lee Gannon, a composer who had struggled against AIDS for more than a decade, was killed in an automobile accident. Bill Monroe, considered the father of bluegrass, also died, prompting a huge outpouring of grief, sorrow, and praise from around the world.

Finally, state officials unveiled a new slogan to attract tourists to Tennessee. Developed by Walker & Associates, considered one of the top public relations firms in the state, it was: "Tennessee. Sounds good to me."

Few were impressed.

YOU ARE SO NASHVILLE IF...

1st Place

You never meant to stay here this long.

—*Robert Jetton*

2nd Place

You look at the pictures of the Gay Pride Parade to see if you know anybody.

—*John Baskett*

3rd Place

You're wondering when Byron Trauger is up for re-election.

—*Randy Johnson*

You're excited to see Turko's face on a milk carton, but you're upset when you find out he's not missing.

—*Gavin Matlock*

You vote for Bill Boner.

—*Dianne Gregory*

honorable mentions

You confess to your husband that you're having an affair, and he wants to know if Mr. Kates is catering.

Pat Wilson

You cried when your daughter went away to college—and it was Vanderbilt.

Bert Knupp

The longest sections in your Yellow Pages are "Churches" and "Escort Services."

Gene Stephens

You dread Adam.

Jan Bell

None of your friends want your back-stage passes to Fan Fair.

—Baxter Buck

The man who wallpapered your office wrote a song that's on The Beatles' *Live From The BBC* album.

—Suzanne Schwalb

You only vote in an election with a pro sports referendum.

—Phillip Cargile

You think using a turn signal drains too much power from your car battery.

—Larry Rumsey

You think you are out really late because the traffic lights are blinking yellow.

—Geneva Brignolo

Your women friends confide that they've screened potential boyfriends by asking them if they've been to Talledega.

—Suzanne Schwalb

You yield the right-of-way to a pedestrian and expect to be thanked.

—*K. Peel*

You've redecorated your trailer so you can rent it out as a bed and breakfast during the Olympics.

—*Gavin Matlock*

You can name seven of the original 100 Oaks stores.

—*Kathy Frost*

You think Brad Schmitt is a gifted journalist.

—*Larry Ramsey*

You'd actually consider Bill Boner again.

—*Gavin Matlock*

You think that's Bud Adams' natural hair.

—*T.R. Carter*

You never had sinus problems until you moved here from another state.

—*Pamela Lanius-Reynolds*

You believe that Jesus turned the water into grapejuice.

—*M. Duncan Currey*

You grew up in Davidson County but you now live in Williamson.

—*Kathy Frost*

You write your best song lyrics on the back of detox unit brochures.

—*M. Duncan Currey*

You think the Gerst Haus should be declared a historical site so it won't be demolished for the new stadium.

—*John Baskett*

You live in Belle Meade, have a net worth of $20 million, and constantly complain that $4.25 an hour is too much to pay the maid.

—*David Tidwell*

Tanya Tucker's husband cuts your lawn.

—*Adam Dread*

You hope the Baptists boycott Opryland so the lines won't be so damn long.

—*Terry Robertson*

You know the plural of "y'all": "All y'all."

—*Tory Sally*

You secretly listen to country music.

—*C. Dean Hughes*

Your local bookstore has a better collection than your main library.

—*Mory Montgomery*

You have an arena with no hockey team and a football team with no stadium.

—*Mary Ann Liden*

You don't read the *Nashville Scene* because you think it's a gay and lesbian publication.

—*Tony Fisher*

You're nice to everyone, even if they *are* going to hell.

—*Terry Robertson*

You take the cellular to church—with the ringer on.

—*Cecilia Eppinger*

You worry more about the fate of the Gerst Haus than you do about that thing over in Bosnia.

—*Eric Davis*

Mayor Bredesen provided tax money for you to move here.

—*Randy Johnson*

You only know where you are in '05 or '15.

—*Billy Webb*

You park in a lot where there used to be a historic building.

—*Randy Johnson*

You can't believe you have to pay for parking downtown.

—*Josh Wells*

You think Trilogy restaurant must be a meat and two.

—*R.F. Smith*

You did not vote "yes" for the stadium because you "don't want Nashville to change," but you're going to vote for Bill Boner because you believe he's a changed man.

—*Tony Binion*

Buster (at Jimmy Kelly's), Mrs. Rotier (at Rotier's), and Paula (at Pancake Pantry) all know you by your first name.

—*Ronnie Steine*

A clerk at Kroger tells you that you can find lox in the hardware aisle.

—*Candace Asher*

You've played chicken with the *General Jackson* riverboat.

—*Denise Volz*

The Party Crowd

From left: **Tony Brown,** MCA mogul, well-dressed man, best possible connection to Vince. **Elise Loehr,** former sommelier (sommelieuse?) Riqué client, best possible connection to Tony Brown. **Chuck Bader,** our man in vodka, king of Absolut, party source (does anybody here remember Jack Daniel's?). **Elizabeth Scokin,** former Arkansan, ubiquitous photographer, source of envy. **Mario Ferrari,** friend of Bud Adams, yachtsman, and—we almost forgot—restaurateur. **Slick Lawson,** photographer, jambalaya meister, sometime royalist. **Anne and Teddy Clayton,** scions of the party bloodline (her from the Sperry's Thomases, him from the fox-trotting Claytons), costume renters, but goodness knows, *never* the last to leave. Photographed by **Slick Lawson,** July 17, 1996.

You've attended first offenders' traffic school more than once.

—*Mary Herron*

You pull over to the side of the road and stop for a funeral procession, but not for an ambulance.

—*Sandra Mannchen*

You put a "God is my co-pilot" bumper sticker on your car instead of learning how to drive.

—*Alex and Kathryn Gorodetzky*

Your best pick-up line is "Hey, wanna get together and write?"

—*Coco Daniel*

You voted for The Olive Garden as Best Italian Restaurant.

—*Linda Hancock*

You put a Christmas wreath on the front of your Land Rover at holiday time.

—*Carol Milam*

You've ever even seen *World News Extra.*

—*Randy Johnson*

You think macaroni and cheese is a vegetable.

—*Linda Hancock*

You'll wait in line for two hours to eat a plate of pancakes.

—*Rachel Yarbrough*

Snow Bird decides when you go Krogering.

—*Beverly Bain*

Your favorite ethnic food and barbecue places are all in Green Hills.

Robert Cogswell

You smell like Brown's Diner.

Dan H. Brawner

You've never actually been to East Nashville, but you just know it's dangerous.

Robert Cogswell

You go out for a home-cooked meal.

Lynn Scarborough

You wear your high school ring instead of your college ring.

—Patsy Curry

You still don't get the H.I.V. lane joke (winner of the 1994 "You Are So Nashville If . . . " contest).

—Alex and Kathryn Gorodetzky

You stand up after every performance, even if it wasn't very good.

—Meredith Jones

You have offspring named Garth or Shania.

—Rachel Yarbrough

Upon hearing news that Krystal was going into bankruptcy, you bought 500 Krystals to put in the freezer.

—David Tidwell

You're planning to chain yourself to the doors of the Gerst Haus when the bull-dozers come.

—Chris Chamberlain

You can't find a place to park at Cummins Station.
—*Tania Owen*

You wish Kay West would move back to New York.
—*Lisa Schmidt*

You think it's normal for women to have names like Peaches and Honey.
—*Alex and Kathryn Gorodetzky*

The bouncer at Robert's Western Wear knows you personally.
—*M. McWhinney*

The primary ingredient of the bird nest in your backyard is discarded audio tape.
—*Glenn Petach*

You took up smoking cigars because Adam Dread says it's cool.
—*Eric Davis*

The Coach

Ed Temple Gentleman, role model, inspiration. Mentor of Wilma Rudolph and the rest of the TSU Tigerbelles. He didn't actually win all those gold medals in the Olympics and the Pan Am games himself, but the honor is all his. Coach Temple wants to donate his memorabilia to the TSU Library. That takes bucks. When he posed for his portrait, he asked to mention that donations are welcome. The pleasure is ours. Photographed by **Michael Gomez** at TSU Library, July 1996.

The Grapes of Wrath

Yikes! We knew folks were miffed when we didn't pick a winner in last year's "You Are So Nashville If..." contest. But we figured that, by now, the wounds would have healed. If this year's entries are any indication, however, you've forgiven Boner, you've forgiven Bredesen, and you've forgiven beer in the arena. But as for the Scene—well, we're still somewhere behind Bud Adams, Turko, Catherine Darnell, Adam Dread, and Planet Hollywood. Don some protective goggles and read these bitter babies:

★ The one year you decide against entering "You Are So Nashville If..." the *Scene* declares no winner.

★ You enter this contest and are shocked, shocked, to discover that someone will actually judge the quality of your work.

★ You make light of your readership's best efforts to make you laugh and then still have the nerve to ask us suckers to play your silly little contest again.

★ You run a copycat entertainment weekly with articles that pander to the mainstream media, then accuse Nashvillians of not being original enough to win your stupid contest.

★ You write for the *Nashville Scene* and consider yourself a real journalist.

★ You work hard to establish a fledgling weekly paper into a significant voice in the satirically deprived Nashville, yet become so self-absorbed that you choose to reproach and patronize your readers instead of laugh with them in a recent "You Are So Nashville If..." contest.

★ Your entire existence cannot be summed up in a two-line sound bite, regardless of the expectations of the *Nashville Scene* editors and contest judges.

★ You actually felt bad that the *Scene* couldn't pick a first-place winner last year. I guess none of us were "Nashville" enough.

★ You're afraid to enter the "You Are So Nashville If..." contest because of last year's scolding the *Nashville Scene* gave its readers for lack of originality.

★ You are still pissed off at the *Nashville Scene* for not naming a winner for this contest last year.

★ You are not embarrassed to live in a city that has a "You Are So Nashville If..." contest.

★ You think you know what is so Nashville.

★ You wonder why they couldn't pick a winner last year.

The Ruling Class

From left: **Alyne Massey** There was a time when she helped write the *Banner*'s society column, but she's moved on. Now she belongs to Suzy, where her name turns up in boldface. It also turns up on the Vanderbilt Law Library, where it's carved in stone. **Clare Armistead** Don't let the wide eyes fool you. This woman is not just here to party. She is here to raise bucks. Big bucks. But she also knows the facts of life: You have to give if you want to receive. **Jane Dudley** Local girl makes good very good. Out of Parmer School and on to the American Embassy in Copenhagen. Back in town, she starts the Swan Ball. Cheekwood is grateful. So is Nashville Tent and Awning. **Lil Granbery** Keeping the list also means keeping the gate. Even at a party for 800, Lil knows, there's not room for *everybody*. Unfortunately, no in-town guests. **Herbert Fox** *N.Focus* editor and available man. When Princess Margaret came to town, Herbert got the call. Of course, he was available, and once again a table was squared, boy-girl, boy-girl. It makes for a busy life. Photographed by **Dee Davis** at Belle Meade Country Club, July 7, 1996.

You don't find it odd to find Paul Harvey on an FM "Cutting Edge of Rock" station.

—Paul Whitfield

You consider Belle Meade Boulevard a tourist attraction to show out-of-town guests.

—Candice Ethridge

You don't exactly know where Antioch is.

—Patsy Curry

You and your wife keep turning the milk carton during breakfast because neither of you wants Turko on your side.

—Rusty Rust

Your children's first names are someone else's last names.

—Patsy Curry

You think BR5-49 plays all originals.

—Bill Owens

Your "historic district" has your city's newest buildings and businesses.

—D.C. Klein

In a drunken stupor, you go up to Johnny Jackson and ask him how Tito and Jermaine are doing.

—Eric Davis

You have your church directory picture made at Glamour Shots.

—Beverly Sears

The Dressers

From left: **A.J. Levy** Suit-and-tie sort of guy. Haberdasher supreme. You do want cuffs on these, don t you? **Katy K.** Kicky, but still country. Kitty Wells on a Really Strange Hair Day. You don t know people who dress like this? Don t worry. They probably don't know you. **Najib** Tammy needs to have a few things taken in. No problem. You mean somebody else already bought it for the ASCAP party? Well, I do think I've seen these bugles before. **Manuel** New-age Nudie. He knows that a little beadwork in just the right places can make even Marty Stuart look tall. Still rockin in his own right. Calvin Klein he is not. Photographed by **Eric England,** July 16, 1996.

The Veterans

Back row, from left: **Stonewall Jackson,** the man who met success at Waterloo. **Porter Wagoner,** who survived Dolly and disco without a hair out of place. **Del Reeves,** still looking at the world through a windshield, *deedle eet deet dee.* **Jimmy C. Newman,** ragin' Cajun and alligator man. **Johnny Russell,** champion of rednecks, white socks, and Blue Ribbon beer. Middle row, from left: **Little Jimmie Dickens,** takin' an old cold 'tater and waitin'. **Grandpa Jones,** *Hee Haw* heartthrob, occasional yodler, suspenders model, now in his eighth decade in showbiz. **Skeeter Davis,** a long way from the end of the world. Front row, from left: **Jack Greene,** the Jolly Green Giant and former Texas Troubadour who built a career on "There Goes My Everything." **"Whispering" Bill Anderson** it's his life, and he'll throw it away if he wants to. **Jeanne Pruett,** who's probably received a warehouse worth of satin sheets from her fans. **Jeannie Seely,** author, singer of "Don't Touch Me," former proprietor of *The Best Little Whorehouse in Texas*—on the Nashville stage, of course. Photographed by **Raeanne Rubenstein** at the Grand Ole Opry House, Friday, July 5, 1996.

You think that the "crack" problem among berry pickers could be solved with properly fitted trousers and suspenders.

—Kenneth Oliver

You still get Christmas cards from Fate Thomas.

—Mack Slayden

When asked "Who does your hair?" you reply, "The front or the back?"

—Riqué

Sometime or another in your life, you've called Blair Boulevard home.

—Amy Adams

You have no problem with living in a city where 21st Avenue intersects with 31st Avenue.

—Eric Teplitz

You keep forgetting that Bill Frist is your senator.

—Eric Davis

You're confused by the ongoing struggle to keep the Nashville Zoo out of Nashville.

—Todd L. Lester

Your preacher thinks the Teddy Bart/Karlen Evins photo is too risqué for a family newspaper.

—Stacy Harris

honorable mentions

You keep a gun in your golf bag and a seven-iron in your gun rack.

Chris Chamberlain

You're just discovering bagels.

Pam Orlando

You're wondering if the Bicentennial Mall has a Gap.

Neil DeWitt

Your society-magazine editor used to write for *Hee Haw*.

Adam Dread

The Albies

★ You love prowling through Bari-Mor for that special something because it reminds you of a cross between your grandmother's attic and the set of a Tennessee Williams play.

★ You love music—all kinds, especially country and western. I believe Nashville music has an up to it all. I know it makes my day. I can feel down and blue, sad, whatever, and listen to good music, and it's a picker-upper. I love being a Nashvillian. I wouldn't want to live anywhere else. The people here are wonderful!

★ You purchase a terrific-looking outfit at a local thrift store for next-to-nothing to wear when you go out for a delicious dinner at one of Nashville's great restaurants with the super discount coupon you clipped from the *Nashville Scene*.

★ You remember Charlotte Pike being two lanes with potholes that would swallow motorcycles; riding the ferry across the Cumberland River out of necessity; having lunch at Centennial Park on the lawn with different Greek gods and goddesses scattered about; enjoying a night at Fair Park, riding the old wooden roller coaster as you scream toward Fourth Avenue.

★ You are loved and understood by the beautiful Nashvillians who are willing to help you looking for a job and a safe place to live with your beloved family. (Writing for hundreds of Vietnamese former POWs in Nashville.)

★ You are smart enough to realize that the heart and soul of this city is music!

★ You're a hopeless romantic who enjoys moonlit strolls, candlelight dinners, evenings by the fireplace, and walks in the rain after TPAC.

★ You throw bread to the ducks at Centennial Park; eat Goo Goos while checking out Second Avenue and Lower Broad; attend at least one Starwood Concert, Opryland Hotel function, a restaurant where celebrities frequent, and a regular religious worshipping site; know someone in the music business and the city government; know what "Athens of the South," Cheekwood, TPAC, Hermitage, Belle Meade Boulevard, and Iroquois signify; know where there are a fort, three museums, and Bicentennial Mall in the city's heart; been to a Swan or Swine-like ball, Grand Ole Opry or Opryland, Italian Street Fair or Summer Lights, Fan Fair or country-music taping; know how to get on/off 440, 265, 65, 24, and 40. Finally, you are so Nashville if you say "you all" like you've lived here all your life.

Your divorce settlement includes your Iroquois box seats.

—Patsy Curry

You first registered to vote while in a sports bar.

—Kathy Wood Robbins

The Do Gooder

Bill Barnes Friend to the downtrodden. Advocate for the oppressed. Champion of justice. Turtleneck-wearing preacher. Retired minister, Edgehill United Methodist Church. Photographer Michael Gomez says he chose the setting for Barnes' portrait because it reminded him of a war trench. There was a nice little bridge in the background. There are times when we have to get in the trenches and build bridges in life. It seems that Rev. Bill Barnes has done it more than most of us. He is a wonderful person. Photographed by **Michael Gomez,** July 1996.

You own at least one outfit that glitters.

—Robin Lawrence

You will ONLY buy a house if it's been inspected by Walter Jowers.

—Rob Biaggi

Your church has a loading dock.

—Jo David and Melissa Keith

You're certain that if Kathy Lee Gifford had stayed a *Hee Haw* Honey, she wouldn't be in this mess right now.

—Robin Lawrence

You can't pull change out of your pocket without sorting through the guitar picks.

—*George Weakley*

You have ever had your hair dyed red by Riqué.

—*Beverly Bain*

You think the folks who line up for Fan Fair are idiots, but you waited in line for eight hours to catch a glimpse of Arnold Schwarzenegger.

—*Karen Hill*

You placed a new Bill Boner bumper sticker over your old one.

—*Paul and Susie Carmichael*

You go to a brew pub and order a Bud Light.

—*Laurence M. Ralston*

Your children's address changes during the school year.

—*Alex and Kathryn Gorodetzky*

honorable mentions

Your child's school looks like a trailer park.

Tracy B. Ann

Last year, you weren't "Nashville" enough.

Robin Lawrence

You know somebody who knows somebody.

Maureen Farley

You claim to love eating sushi but only order California rolls.

John Baeder

1997

It was a hard year to figure. Maybe, just maybe, we were beginning to have doubts about whether we really wanted to be the big city we had become.

The number of homicides in Nashville in 1997 broke all existing records. Gripped by a crime panic, the mayor established a blue-ribbon commission of city leaders who grappled with the crime wave.

Meanwhile, many Nashvillians were rejoicing about getting a real, live, National Football League team to play in a new East-bank stadium, just as many of us were griping about the owner, Bud Adams, who seemed to need a lesson or two in public relations. First, Adams said he would change the team's name from the Oilers to something else. Then, just as quickly, Adams said he had lived with the name for years and didn't want to change it. Attendance at Oilers games in the Liberty Bowl in Memphis was pitifully low. On Sunday afternoons, television sportscasters spoke in awe of the record-low attendance marks.

The biggest national story taking place in our very midst was often out of public view. Inside the corporate offices at Columbia/HCA, the nation's healthcare giant, federal agents were conducting a mammoth sweep to determine if the company had swindled the nation's Medicare program. Amid the glare of negative publicity from the front pages of *The New York Times* and from other media, company president Rick Scott was sacked. HCA founder Tom Frist was named as Scott's successor.

As the city boomed, the club scene rocked, unemployment reached record lows, and traffic became a nightmare of miasmic proportions. But as state planners worked on expanding an interstate ring to surround Davidson County, environmentalists and rural residents howled. They didn't want to become part of the suburban sprawl that was so evidently gobbling up every other part of the metropolitan area.

Meanwhile, Perry March—attorney, father, and a man never charged in the death of his wife, Janet Levine March—opened up a law office in Nashville. He never showed up for work and instead moved to the Chicago area, where his family lives. Obviously, he wasn't much wanted in Music City.

You are so Nashville if...

1st Place

You've checked your flower bed for Janet March.

—*Terry Robertson*

2nd Place

Your arena has a steeple.

—*Ron Kidd*

3rd Place

Your dining guide has an entire section devoted to catfish.

—*Pam Orlando*

4th Place

You think Perry March should be Paul Reid's attorney.

—*John Baskett*

5th Place

You've ever seen DaVido throw a hissy fit.

—*Chris Chamberlain*

You went to the big Vandy/Notre Dame game just to hear Joe Diffie sing the national anthem.

—*Karla Frank*

You could understand a conversation between Street Talk Shorty and the Emma's flowers guy.

—*Robert Cogswell*

You date past events as being before or after "the big ice storm."

—*Alice Fitzgibbon*

You've ever fantasized about blowing the Nashville Trolley off the road.

—*Karla Frank*

You don't own a computer, but you just got your own web site with CitySearch.

—*Jill Vick*

honorable mentions

You think "Noshville" is a misprint.

Todd Truley

You've worked at Gibson for at least a month.

Tami Heinbach

You know someone who's having a house delivered.

Cary Beare

You put jelly on a bagel.

Diana Hecht and Katie Patton

You're still waiting for 25-cent-beer-night at the symphony.

—*Eric Tichenor*

You think "Bud and Phil" refers to the Everly Brothers.

—*John Furgess*

You're introduced to someone and the first thing they say is, "I know your father."

—*Lucius Carroll III*

You've ever gotten a speeding ticket from a bicycle cop.

—*Paul D. Chrisman*

You have ever petted one of the pony statues at the Wildhorse Saloon.

—*Faye Walker*

Your favorite seafood is hush puppies.

—*Sharon Anderson*

You think Connie really *does* go out.

—*Matt Milligan*

You settle your civil disputes at Amateur Boxing Night at the Mix Factory.

—*Chris Chamberlain*

You believe Jerry Falwell autographs Mickey Mouse posters at Opryland just to get a season pass.

—*Jeffrey Hargis*

You think 770-Puck is a sex-pervert call-in line.

—*Garner Allred*

You wish Rudy Kalis would run away with Ava Harvey.

—*Hank-Bob Schmidt*

You believe Jerry Falwell autographs Mickey Mouse posters at Opryland just to get a season pass.

—*Jeffrey Hargis*

The Baptist boycott of Disney popped up in a Sunday sermon, and you go to the Church of Christ!

—*Joseph C. Estes Jr.*

honorable mentions

You didn't mind going to Kentucky for phen-fen because it gave you an excuse to buy lottery tickets.

Greg Denton

You tie your old shoes together and throw them over a phone wire.

Amy Yarbro

You think Church Street Centre could be the first library in the country with its own food court.

John J. Brassil

A Distinctly Nashville Moment

I think I was actually in Memphis when I had one of those moments of understanding about Nashville. I was sitting in a restaraunt with some Memphis acquaintances, and there was some country music playing in the background. One of them remarked, "The thing I couldn't stand about living in Nashville would be having to listen to all that country music all the time." Of course, the thing that dawned on me then was that you really don't hear that much of it in Nashville. We may be selling it, but it isn't that much a part of the private lives of individual Nashvillians.

Phil Ashford,
policy advisor to
Metro Mayor Phil Bredesen

★

You can properly mispronounce the name "Lafayette."

—*Ruth P. Cunningham*

You don't know how we got by before Stormtracker 2000.

—*Pam Orlando*

You spend Sunday afternoon at the Brentwood Harris Teeter store just to see what it will be like when it comes to Belle Meade.

—*Gilbert Foster*

After the property assessment, your moving sale sign said "Build it and we will leave."

—*Kathy Grace*

You consider abortion to be wrong, but you think capital punishment is OK.

—*Greg Denton*

You've nominated Crom Carmicheal for a Sunshine Award.

—*Jeff Wilson*

You know what it means when somebody says, "It works if you hold your mouth right."

—*Kathy Grace*

You pass up the 50-cent *Banner* to get a free copy of the *Scene*.

—*Ace Anthony*

You've always wanted to live in a $200,000 house, and now, thanks to the tax assessor's office, you do.

—*Lory Montgomery*

Your legislator cares more about what Darwin said about you than what the rest of the country thinks about you.

—*Greg Denton*

You own a Land Rover and you *still* won't drive in the snow.

—*Pam Orlando*

You're still ticked off at the *Scene* for not picking a winner two years ago.

—*Joseph C. Estes Jr.*

You've even *considered* naming the new hockey team "The Snowbirds."

—*Jeff Wilson*

A Distinctly Nashville Moment

[*N.Focus* editor] Herbert Fox and I lived on the same street when we were kids, four houses apart. In grade school, he got the award for being the best writer. I remember going to his house and watching him write. He was left-handed, and he had wonderful handwriting. He was a fabulous writer. He and Teenie, my sister, are best friends. His mother and my mother were best friends. That *N.Focus* is in focus. That's a terrific publication. It's better than the *Nashville Scene*.

John Jay Hooker, attorney/entrepreneur/ political reformer

★

You've considered walking through Church Street Centre nude but were afraid no one would be there to see you.
—*Greg Denton*

There's a festive theme to your yard sale.
—*Glenn Petach*

Your pastor spends 10 minutes on a Sunday morning explaining that church is *not* the proper place to pass audition tapes.

—*Steve Lawlor*

You call WKDF and ask Dook and Big Dave for relationship advice.
—*Scott Wollschlager*

You buy your clothes at Jamie and shop for your children at Target.
—*Matt Milligan*

You don't get out of your house during legislative session because you know Sen. Harold Ford's in town.

—*Syd Lovelace*

You're afraid to wear your Mickey Mouse watch to church.

—Michael Manly

You wish there were a summertime movie in which dinosaurs escaped from Grassmere, stomped the arena, and ate Mayor Bredesen.

—Garner Allred

Your subdivision sponsors a weekly writers' night.

—Keith A. Gordon

You thought the Macarena was a foreign country.

—Debbie Williams

You do everything "in the round."

—Rish James

You believe that a man accused of committing seven fast-food murders could have cut a better demo tape, and you are the one who could have done it.

—Ed Norris

A Distinctly Nashville Moment

I got my first set of tails for a high school dance. That's what we did back then. We all wore tails, and we passed them down from one boy to the next. I think our mothers must have had some sort of exchange. I remember that I had Frank Berry's. We all wanted to be so sophisticated, but I was grown up and living in New York before I realized how stupid we were. Can you see Ed Nelson at 13, short as he is, dressed in tails? It was ludicrous. He looked like a penguin.

Herbert Fox, inveterate man-about-town and editor of N.Focus

You called Crime Stoppers about Paul Reid.

—*Lola and Suzanne Austin*

You used to watch Channel 4 for Demetria but now switch between Amy on 5 and Victoria on 2.

—*Joseph C. Estes Jr.*

"Meat and Three" is what you call your husband and kids.

—*Ellen Pierce*

You heard that Demi Moore was going to be at Planet Hollywood and went because you like beef stew.

—*Greg Denton*

"Diversity" means having more than one Target.

—*Matt Milligan*

You simply *adore* Rebecca Bain.

—*Jonathan Riggs*

Your downtown historic district was founded in 1996.

—*Rish James*

You pronounce Demonbreun with three M's.

—*Stephanie Juste, also John Rumble*

CAN I GET TO MUR·FREEZ·BOR·OH BY GETTING ON LAH·FEE·YET OR DEEMON·BREWIN?

You've replaced your "I Miss Ned" bumper sticker with one that says "I Miss Peaches."

—*Rusty DeGraff*

Your attorney is suspected of having committed a worse crime than you have.

—*Morris Brown*

You go to the downtown library, even when you don't need a quiet place to sleep off a drunk.

—*Greg Denton*

Eric Crafton is your favorite guitarist.

—*Stacy Harris*

You have a bonus room over the garage.

—*Matt Milligan*

You hold a bake sale to reopen Hap Townes.

—*Lory Montgomery*

You have columns on your log house.

—*Ron Kidd*

A Distinctly Nashville Moment

About a year and a half ago, I was driving my Peterbilt down Gallatin Road near Ma & Pa's Bar. All of a sudden, I looked over and saw this naked man walking down the street. This woman was about to pull out into traffic, and she looked over and saw the naked man. I don't know why, but she throws her car in reverse and starts flying backwards down the street about 50 mph. She didn't even look in the rearview mirror. When you see people driving the way they do in Nashville, consider this: They may have a reason.

Phil Lee, singer/truck driver

A Distinctly Nashville Moment

I played with Jimmy Church on *Night Train*, the first black TV show in Nashville. Jimmy Church was about as cool as they come; he was a good singer, charming. Women were crazy about him. He was like Jackie Wilson at the time. That was Nashville music, and music is what Nashville means to me. Then there was the time Jimi Hendrix came lookin' to cut my head, as the saying goes, as the top-dog guitarist in town.

Johnny Jones, guitarist and proprietor of Modern Era night club

You still complain about the arena and the stadium.

—John Baskett

You feverishly opposed the Houston Oilers coming to Nashville but bought a PSL, just in case.

—Tom Catron

You're not sure why downtown needs a new library when it already has the "World's Largest Adult Bookstore."

—Greg Denton

You've just caused a fender bender and your excuse is "I thought you went."

—Maureen Kelly

You can say that the mechanical bull has "been done."

—Carrie Smith and Addie Hill

Your legislator wants to speed up handgun permits, just in case he needs to wave one at a truck driver on I-40.

—Greg Denton

You try to pay for something, and the only change you've got in your pocket is guitar picks.

—*Terry Kinakin*

You put your kids back into public schools to pay for your PSLs.

—*Mark Mott*

You think Watkins Institute is a drug rehab center.

—*Syd Lovelace*

You've ever gotten into an argument with Burger King Betty next to SATCO.

—*Todd Hurst*

You don't mind people drinking within 85 feet of your church—as long as they pay to park in your church parking lot.

—*Mike Brown*

You intend to pay for your child's college education with the dividends from your Beanie Baby investment.

—*Timothy Neal Templeton*

A Distinctly Nashville Moment

I can remember being a newcomer in Nashville's radio and TV business. I was doing whatever I was asked, watching Judd Collins, Dave Overton, Larry Munson, and the other consummate professionals who were part of the WSM radio and television stable of personalities in the '60s. And I was dreaming that I could one day be like them.

Teddy Bart, host of WKDA-AM's Roundtable talk show

★

A Distinctly Nashville Moment

When I was going all over the county campaigning, one day I was at the Jackson Street Baptist Church. They had a program where a little girl was to give a talk. She got up and started, but she just couldn't do it. She had to sit down. So, after that, every adult who got up to speak instinctively told stories about something they had done that was a mess-up, something that had not worked out, and they all said it was OK. They never said anything directly to her. But it was just a powerful affirmation of that child. It was a very Nashville thing.

Betty C. Nixon, former mayoral candidate and Metro Council member, now special assistant for university relations and general counsel at Vanderbilt University

You're moving to New Zealand, New York, or Savannah.

—Tania Owen

You don't read the *Scene* because you saw "Albie Del Favero" on the masthead and figured it was Mafia-owned.

—Chris Chamberlain

You wonder why there are so many Japanese people living in Smyrna.

—Joseph Maness

You use your daughter's body to sell pools and spas on local television.

—Chuck Jones

You've ever lusted after the Watson's Pool girl.

—Philip R. Cloutier

You think Willy Stern's next investigation will focus on why Brad Schmitt gets so much vacation time from *The Tennessean*.

—Stacy Harris

You wonder where all the people are who used to go to Woodmont Baptist on TV.

—*Joseph C. Estes Jr.*

Any part of your car is held together with duct tape.

—*Tracy Ann*

You believe the world would be a much better place if only the Jews and Disney would see things your way.

—*Ira Rogers*

You think Bud Adams is a Southern microbrew.

—*Joe Scutella*

You would have gone ahead and just eaten the Nun Bun.

—*Philip R. Cloutier*

You saw the Nun Bun but didn't know who Mother Teresa was.

—*Diana Hecht and Katie Patton*

Your boss has a secret Kay West contingency plan.

—*Jason Miller*

You want to know why Nashville needs a hockey team, since there are already enough people in town with missing teeth.

—*Garner Allred*

The Albies

★ You stop and lend a hand, even to a total stranger. You say, "Hello, how are you doing?" (and really want to know). I grew up outside of Tennessee, and the first thing I noticed was the friendliness and helpful people. I do customer service and hear all the time how nice and polite (yes ma'am, no sir) we Southerners are. It's true!!

★ You love God, country music, city and country, symphonies, plays, arts, crafts, hills, villages, happiness, sadness, sun, clouds, rain, birds, squirrels, for God made it *all*.

★ You can remember Shelby Park as a "family setting": paddle boats, feeding the ducks, banana popsicles, safe playgrounds, laughter. Let's bring that back—my parents practically grew up there.

★ You remember when you could climb the iron steps of the Capitol and go up in the steeple and sit down.

★ You still think it's a shame what they've done to the Belle Meade Theater.

★ You can fill in the blanks: "Take home a package of ____", "Sing it over and over and over again, ____", "At Happy Day we clean your clothes the soft-set way with ____."

* You bought birthday presents at Belle Meade Hardware and had the birthday party at Pie's Party House (a guest house in Harding Place).

* You take Nashville as it is— good or bad.

* The restaurants you dined in were: Candyland (downtown), Nero's, Belle Meade Motel, and Jimmy Kelly's (in the basement).

* You remember when the old Sam Davis Hotel was about the tallest building in town, and you could not see it if you were two blocks away for all the smoke and soot flying in the air in the mornings.

* You volunteered a lot of time to help get the Nashville Grassmere Zoo built so that everyone can enjoy it, the animals and all. I did 33 and a half hours and I'm disabled, so everyone could help out. I'm also 63 and a half.

* You're a baby boomer who once dared to sneak a ride on one of the brightly painted carousel horses anchored in Fred Harvey's "store-that-never-knew-completion" on Church Street, or every Christmas shivered in the cold to gawk at the bathed-in-blue-light nativity scene mounted by Harvey's Department Store along the Parthenon's south facade.

You'll drive across town for brown paper grocery bags with handles.

—*Kimberly Kimbrough*

You can remember when Fountain Square and Church Street Centre actually had stores.

—*Greg Denton*

You hope that one day you'll be mentioned in "Brad About You."

—*Philip R. Cloutier*

You don't see anything wrong with the name Nashville State Technical Institute.

—*Kris Massey*

You say one thing but mean another.

—*Greg Naas*

You own a Tie-Dye Mary.

—*Gerry Findley*

You end insulting remarks with "bless his heart."

—*Diana Hecht and Katie Patton*

You still raise chickens within the city limits.

—*Greg Naas*

You haven't figured out whose side you're on in the Conway Twitty family debacle.

—*Rusty DeGraff*

You go to Blockbuster Music to listen to the CD, but you go to Tower to buy it.

—*Gerry Findley*

You seriously thought about leaving Tennessee unless phen-fen was legalized.

—*Philip R. Cloutier*

You wash your phen-fen down with a bottle of Yoo-Hoo.

—*Bill Herrick*

Your wardrobe is black, your hair is blond, and your nails are acrylic.

—*Judy Baldridge*

You're voted "Best New Restaraunt," only to close right away.

—*Diana Hecht and Katie Patton*

The guy sitting next to you in an AA meeting is writing a country song.

—*David Dobson*

You get excited because a new grocery store came to town.

—*Robin Cohn*

Your full name can be reversed and still make sense.

—*Diana Hecht and Katie Patton*

Turko reminds you of a young Chris Clark.

—*John Heacock*

You've been bought out by Gaylord Entertainment.

—*Chad Young*

A Distinctly Nashville Moment

I went to the Guns 'n Roses concert at Starwood when they opened for Lynyrd Skynyrd. I'm waiting for some friends, and I see two guys kind of staring at each other, and there's a girl next to each of them. All of a sudden, one girl says to the other, "You f....d my boyfriend!" She grabbed the back of the other girl's head, and they started going at it. All these people started to gather round, and while the girls were fighting, I noticed the two guys were standing next to each other, laughing. It's like they were communing with each other, watching the women duke it out.

*Craig Brabson,
visual artist*

You were thrilled to hear that Lorianne Crook and Charlie Chase were moving back.

—*T. Wallace*

You've been fired by Speer Communications or Tuned In Broadcasting.

—*Amanda Cantrell Roche*

Your favorite place to visit is Bart Durham's web site.

—*M. Skinner*

Your street has a first, middle, and last name.

—*Suzanne Price*

You miss Ned.

—*Charles A. Ervin*

You vacation in Alabama.

—*Ellen Pierce*

You refer to your 1,000-plus church congregation as "small, but growing..."

—*Meg McWhinney*

You personally seek out Catherine Darnell at a party and pretend you're just making small talk.

—*Amy Wedlund*

When the Belcourt Theater showed *The Horseman on the Roof*, you hoped he was there to fix it.

—*Jeanette DeMain*

You think we "needed the rain."

—*Diana Hecht and Katie Patton*

Helen at Village Cleaners knows your name.

—*Philip R. Cloutier*

Your minister has used NASCAR, golf, or pro-wrestling analogies in his sermons.

—*Philip R. Cloutier*

You look forward to Bredesen stepping down as mayor so you and your cousins can run the town again.

—*Syd Lovelace*

You think MDHA is actually going to follow Christine Kreyling's suggestions.

—*Rusty DeGraff*

You have bruised kneecaps from those danged cup holders at the arena.

—*Joseph C. Estes Jr.*

Your idea of recreating an urban neighborhood is to build a 23-story apartment highrise.

—*Pam Orlando*

Views of the Weird

Sometimes a "You Are So Nashville" entry defies explanation. Sometime's it's just like a poem. It doesn't have to mean anything. It just is.

As proof that running this contest is like striking a pact with Satan, we present a selection of entries so curious they gave us pause. They also gave us a case of the hives.

If you understand any of this, please keep it to yourself.

YOU ARE SO WEIRDLY NASHVILLE IF...

★ You are wondering who is going to pay for the stadium if Bud asks for something, "is turned down," and walks before his 30-year lease is up. We could just change the rules like on the arena and sell alcohol in the back door of the church. It happened and could happen again "to keep Bud here."

★ You've "been there-done that," with family and friends who live out of state. We visit all the same attractions Nashville has to offer. Each time someone comes to visit, they ask, "What is there to do?" Here we go again!

★ You have figured out why we are called HILLBILLIES (BULLIES): instead of MUSIC CITY MOUNTAINEERS. OUR CITY FATHERS (politicians) got THEIR CART BEFORE THE HORSES and OVERSTEPPED THE TRACE CHAINS (VOTER PATIENCE and TAX HIKE LIMITS)!

★ You almost fall through a Metro sewer grate and there's no football player to pull you out.

★ Note to Note, the tune from the Soul and the Music of the Heart, beats a rhythm and collects an inspirational vision of a child who turns into a man with courage, honor, and wisdom of truth!!

★ Your name is "Tootsie," your sermons are delivered by "Percy Priest," you only drink "Spring Water," were born in L.A., are confused by *The Tennessean/Nashville Banner*, and think the word "gourmet" should be on the Brown's Diner sign.

★ You think the craters caused by the water company's access cover in the tire-tread sections of Nashville's roads are there to simulate the streets of Paris-Roubaix.

★ All it takes is for one special someone to believe in you. He who believes in him puts his fate in his hands.

★ As an ardent disciple of the city's only Theravada Buddhist monk, you discover with dismay that he hopes to be reincarnated as a country singer. (This sounds absurd, but it is absolutely true.)

★ Your city's 200 is in another town.

★ You grew up on the wrong side of the wrong side of the tracks, halfway between Hopewell and Needmore. When you made it big, you moved to Rayon City from Dupontonia, after getting a Ph.D. at Jordonia.

Views of the Weird

★ The only time you don't sleep naked is after fumigating the house.

★ You see children of any national origin playing together or just hang-outing at a game or purchasing goods at the mall or store, responsibly.

★ Ewe no nasvil be ah madejor leege cidy cose we got prow sportz, cus yer publik skool techer sed soo!

★ You see signs that say Jo Johnston, Jefferson Street, Buchanan, and end up on Clarksville Highway, simply because you made the wrong turn on 18th from Charlotte. Not a tourist attraction?

★ *You left your job of 20 years, your family, your dog with big, droopy ears, bought yourself the most expensive guitar, came to Nashville to become a Star, 6 months later that's not what you are, for 20 bucks you have hocked your guitar, now on the corner of Music Row and exit 209, "Will Work For Food," that's what it says on your sign, you would settle for money to get a cheap bottle of wine, but you would like your friends back home to know, you've finally made it and can be seen daily on Music Row!*

★ You think that you're someone that you're not.

★ *Sleeping under bridges,*
Eating twice a week.
Smoke 'em if you got 'em;
Hope the box don't leak.

Road crew come to clear us out;
Eye-sores that we are.
Tear our tents down,
take us down-town
In their po-lice car.

Take us to the mission
with all the other "bums,"
Sleeping something wicked off...
Pray tomorrow never comes.

Move it on to... Memphis?
(Yeah, RIGHT!)
Anywhere but here.
Be somebody else's trouble
A million days a year.

Two weeks' walk to Louisville ...
sure, THAT sounds like fun.
Pardon me, there Officer...
Can I borrow your GUN?

★ You are a Damn Yankee of 10 years, and you love it here, like I do. If you need a charge, just drive down Battery Lane. Watch it, you may blow up. Happy Fourth to all.

★ You are a man out of work and luck, who stands on a bridge at a light, holding a guitar in one hand and a sign in the other that reads "Please help, I'm pregnant and need food," and the sign is upside down!

★ You're at Second Story Cafe, waiting for an appointment in Green Hills. Between sips of latte, you pass the time reading *The Tennessean* obits—who wins *today*, "cause of death not disclosed," or "injuries sustained in auto accident"?